KT-501-625

Timesavers for Teachers, Book 1

Interactive Classroom Forms and Essential Tools, with CD

Stevan Krajnjan

WS 2262608 5

7-2004

TES

UNIVERSITY OF CHICHESTER

Copyright © 2001, 2003, 2009 by Stevan Krajnjan. All rights reserved.

Published by Jossey-Bass
A Wiley Imprint
989 Market Street, San Francisco, CA 94103-1741—www.josseybass.com

No part of this publication may be reproduced, stored in a retrieval system, or transmitted in any form or by any means, electronic, mechanical, photocopying, recording, scanning, or otherwise, except as permitted under Section 107 or 108 of the 1976 United States Copyright Act, without either the prior written permission of the publisher, or authorization through payment of the appropriate per-copy fee to the Copyright Clearance Center, Inc., 222 Rosewood Drive, Danvers, MA 01923, 978-750-8400, fax 978-646-8600, or on the Web at www.copyright.com. Requests to the publisher for permission should be addressed to the Permissions Department, John Wiley & Sons, Inc., 111 River Street, Hoboken, NJ 07030, 201-748-6011, fax 201-748-6008, or online at www.wiley.com/go/permissions.

Readers should be aware that Internet Web sites offered as citations and/or sources for further information may have changed or disappeared between the time this was written and when it is read.

Limit of Liability/Disclaimer of Warranty: While the publisher and author have used their best efforts in preparing this book, they make no representations or warranties with respect to the accuracy or completeness of the contents of this book and specifically disclaim any implied warranties of merchantability or fitness for a particular purpose. No warranty may be created or extended by sales representatives or written sales materials. The advice and strategies contained herein may not be suitable for your situation. You should consult with a professional where appropriate. Neither the publisher nor author shall be liable for any loss of profit or any other commercial damages, including but not limited to special, incidental, consequential, or other damages.

Jossey-Bass books and products are available through most bookstores. To contact Jossey-Bass directly call our Customer Care Department within the U.S. at 800-956-7739, outside the U.S. at 317-572-3986, or fax 317-572-4002.

Jossey-Bass also publishes its books in a variety of electronic formats. Some content that appears in print may not be available in electronic books.

ISBN: 978-0-4703-9532-5

Library of Congress catalog information available from publisher

Printed in the United States of America

FIRST EDITION

PB Printing   10 9 8 7 6 5 4 3 2 1

372
110
2
KRA

Table of Contents

To my family Ana, Laura, Leah, and Lucas Krajnjan

About This Book

This book is a complete collection of often-used, printable, interactive, classroom forms that are designed to help teachers simplify work, personal organization, record keeping, and classroom management. The interactive CD included makes it possible for you to type information directly on the forms, save and/or print the file, modify information, and access it with ease.

The forms are self-explanatory, easy to understand, and ready to copy or print. Some of the forms have several similar but different versions, as they reflect the variety of different schools, timetables, settings, and situations that teachers may experience. To make the material work for you, simply choose and use one of the forms and the included organizational materials that best fit your current situation and personal classroom needs.

This valuable timesaving tool will keep working for you for many years to come, no matter what your teaching situation or how many times it changes.

Free yourself from the time-consuming burden of having to create your own classroom administrative forms from scratch. Be a well-organized and better prepared teacher by using this book, and have more time for other things in life!

And if you find these forms helpful, you might also like *Timesavers for Teachers, Book 2: Report Card and IEP Comments, Substitute Teacher Instruction kit, and Classroom Awards and Passes, with CD,* also from Jossey-Bass Teacher, available at local bookstores and online retailers.

About the Author

Over his extensive teaching career, Stevan Krajnjan has learned that teaching is a complex job, and time a very precious commodity for every educator. It became obvious to him early on that busy teachers are always looking for ways to lessen the ever-increasing demand on their professional and personal time. This observation led Stevan to develop his popular, often-used materials that help teachers become well-organized, better prepared, and—most importantly—leave them with more time. These materials were first introduced on his Web site: timesaversforteachers.com, and are now available in this and other Timesavers for Teachers books.

Stevan attended McMaster University where he played varsity tennis and graduated with a Bachelor of Arts degree. He received his Bachelor of Education degree from University of Toronto and acquired Specialist qualifications in Computers in the Classroom and Special Education. A full-time teacher since 1985, Stevan teaches Special Education in Brampton, Ontario, Canada, where he resides with his wife, Ana, and their three children, Laura, Lucas, and Leah. In 1997 Stevan was presented with an Exceptional Teacher Award by The Learning Disabilities Association of Mississauga and North Peel in recognition for outstanding work with children with learning disabilities.

In addition to teaching and designing timesaving teacher resources, Stevan enjoys dabbling in art and competing in provincial tennis tournaments. Stevan was a provincially ranked tennis player throughout the last 30 years. In recognition of his sports accomplishments, Stevan was recently inducted into the *City of Brampton Sports Hall of Fame.*

For more information on Stevan and his timesavers, see www.timesaversforteachers.com.

Introduction

This book is a complete collection of often-used, printable, interactive, classroom forms that help teachers simplify work, personal organization, record keeping, and classroom management. The interactive version makes it possible for teachers to type information directly on the forms, save the file, modify information, and access it with ease.

Its pages are visually pleasing, self-explanatory, easy to understand, and ready to print. Some of the forms have several similar but different versions, as they reflect the variety of different school, timetable settings, and situations that teachers may experience throughout their long teaching career. To make the material work for you, simply choose and use the forms and the included organizational materials that best fit your current situation and personal classroom needs. Teachers find the content of this book useful and relevant, even when their grade levels and teaching assignments are changed. It is a valuable timesaving tool that will keep working for you for many more years to come.

To use this book effectively, it is suggested that individual pages are printed, as needed, directly from the computer. If photocopying is the cheaper and preferred option, print the book in its entirety, place the pages in a three-ring binder, insert the binder spine label and the title page on the outside, and then photocopy individual pages, as needed, throughout the school year. Creating a portable three-ring binder of timesaving forms and included resources makes access, reference, and use always practical and easy.

Free yourself from the time-consuming burden of having to create your own classroom administrative forms from scratch. Be a well-organized and better prepared teacher by using this book . . . and have more time for other things in life!

IMPORTANT Events Calendar

DATE	EVENT	NOTES

Copyright © 2001, 2003, 2009 by Stevan Krajnjan

Important Events Calendar

DATE	EVENT	NOTES

Copyright © 2001, 2003, 2009 by Stevan Krajnjan

The Teacher's Binder

CALENDAR TEMPLATE

Month: _____

Sun	Mon	Tue	Wed	Thu	Fri	Sat

Copyright © 2001, 2003, 2009 by Stevan Krajnjan

Long-Range Plans

MONTH	SUBJECT	SUBJECT
☞		

Copyright © 2001, 2003, 2009 by Stevan Krajnjan

Long-Range Plans

MONTH	SUBJECT	SUBJECT

Copyright © 2001. 2003. 2009 by Stevan Krajnjan

 **TIMETABLE**

Semester/Term: _____

Room: _____

	Day 1	Day 2	Day 3	Day 4	Day 5	Day 6	Day 7

Copyright © 2001, 2003, 2009 by Stevan Krajnjan

The Teacher's Binder

 **TIMETABLE**

Semester/Term: _____

Room: _____

	Day 1	Day 2	Day 3	Day 4	Day 5	Day 6

Copyright © 2001, 2003, 2009 by Stevan Krajnjan

TEACHER TIMETABLE

Semester/Term: _____

Room: _____

Copyright © 2001, 2003, 2009 by Stevan Krajnjan

The Teacher's Binder

TIMETABLE

Semester/Term: _____

Room: _____

Copyright © 2001, 2003, 2009 by Stevan Krajnjan

TIMETABLE

Semester/Term: _____

Room: _____

Copyright © 2001. 2003. 2009 by Stevan Krajnjan

 **TIMETABLE**

Semester/Term: _____

Room: _____

Copyright © 2001. 2003. 2009 by Stevan Krajnjan

Teacher Timetable

	Day 1	Day 2	Day 3	Day 4	Day 5	Day 6	Day 7
Period 1							
Period 2							
Period 3							
LUNCH !							
Period 4							
Period 5							
Period 6							

Dismissal, Lockers, Remedial, Detention, Extracurricular Activities:

Copyright © 2001, 2003, 2009 by Stevan Krajnjan

Teacher Timetable

Name: _____

Room: _____

Class: _____

	Day 1	Day 2	Day 3	Day 4	Day 5	Day 6	Day 7
Period 1							
Period 2							
Period 3							
Period 4							
LUNCH !							
Period 5							
Period 6							

Dismissal, Lockers, Remedial, Detention, Extracurricular Activities:

Copyright © 2001, 2003, 2009 by Stevan Krajnjan

Teacher Timetable

Name: _____
Room: _____
Class: _____

	Day 1	Day 2	Day 3	Day 4	Day 5	Day 6
Period 1						
Period 2						
Period 3						
LUNCH !						
Period 4						
Period 5						
Period 6						

Dismissal, Lockers, Remedial, Detention, Extracurricular Activities:

Copyright © 2001, 2003, 2009 by Stevan Krajnjan

The Teacher's Binder

Teacher Timetable

Name: _____
Room: _____
Class: _____

	Day 1	Day 2	Day 3	Day 4	Day 5	Day 6
Period 1						
Period 2						
Period 3						
Period 4						
LUNCH !						
Period 5						
Period 6						

Dismissal, Lockers, Remedial, Detention, Extracurricular Activities:

Copyright © 2001, 2003, 2009 by Stevan Krajnjan

Teacher Timetable

LUNCH !

Dismissal, Lockers, Remedial, Detention, Extracurricular Activities:

Copyright © 2001, 2003, 2009 by Stevan Krajnjan

Teacher Timetable

Name: _____
Room: _____
Class: _____

LUNCH !

Dismissal, Lockers, Remedial, Detention, Extracurricular Activities:

Copyright © 2001. 2003. 2009 by Stevan Krajnjan

Teacher Timetable

LUNCH !

Dismissal, Lockers, Remedial, Detention, Extracurricular Activities:

Copyright © 2001, 2003, 2009 by Stevan Krajnjan

Teacher Timetable

Name: _____

Room: _____

Class: _____

LUNCH !

Dismissal, Lockers, Remedial, Detention, Extracurricular Activities:

Copyright © 2001. 2003. 2009 by Stevan Krajnjan

School *Timetable*

Name: _____

Room: _____

Class: _____

☼	Day 1	Day 2	Day 3	Day 4	Day 5	Day 6	Day 7
Period 1							
Period 2							
Period 3							
LUNCH !							
Period 4							
Period 5							
Period 6							

Dismissal, Lockers, Remedial, Detention, Extracurricular Activities:

Copyright © 2001, 2003, 2009 by Stevan Krajnjan

The Teacher's Binder

School Timetable

Name: _____

Room: _____

Class: _____

	Day 1	Day 2	Day 3	Day 4	Day 5	Day 6	Day 7
Period 1							
Period 2							
Period 3							
Period 4							
LUNCH !							
Period 5							
Period 6							

Dismissal, Lockers, Remedial, Detention, Extracurricular Activities:

Copyright © 2001, 2003, 2009 by Stevan Krajnjan

School Timetable

Name: _____

Room: _____

Class: _____

	Day 1	Day 2	Day 3	Day 4	Day 5	Day 6
Period 1						
Period 2						
Period 3						
LUNCH !						
Period 4						
Period 5						
Period 6						

Dismissal, Lockers, Remedial, Detention, Extracurricular Activities:

Copyright © 2001, 2003, 2009 by Stevan Krajnjan

School Timetable

Copyright © 2001, 2003, 2009 by Stevan Krajnjan

Name: _____

Room: _____

Class: _____

	Day 1	Day 2	Day 3	Day 4	Day 5	Day 6
Period 1						
Period 2						
Period 3						
Period 4						
LUNCH !						
Period 5						
Period 6						

Dismissal, Lockers, Remedial, Detention, Extracurricular Activities:

School Timetable

	Time
School Entry	
National Anthem, Announcements	
Homeroom/Home Form	
LUNCH	
After-Lunch School Entry	
Period **1**	
Period **2**	
Period **3**	
Period **4**	
Period **5**	
Period **6**	
Period **7**	
Period **8**	
School Dismissal	
Remedial help, Extracurricular activities	
Duty:	

Copyright © 2001, 2003, 2009 by Stevan Krajnjan

School Timetable

	Time
School Entry	
National Anthem, Announcements	
Homeroom/ Home Form	
LUNCH	
After-Lunch School Entry	
Period **1**	
Period **2**	
Period **3**	
Period **4**	
Period **5**	
Period **6**	
School Dismissal	
Remedial help, Extracurricular activities	
Duty:	

Copyright © 2001, 2003, 2009 by Stevan Krajnjan

STUDENT TIMETABLE

Semester/Term: _____

Room: _____

	Day 1	Day 2	Day 3	Day 4	Day 5	Day 6	Day 7
Period							
Period							
Period							
Period							
Period							
Period							
Period							
Period							

Copyright © 2001. 2003. 2009 by Stevan Krajnjan

TIMETABLE

Semester/Term: _____

Room: _____

	Day 1	Day 2	Day 3	Day 4	Day 5	Day 6
Period						
Period						
Period						
Period						
Period						
Period						
Period						
Period						

Copyright © 2001, 2003, 2009 by Stevan Krajnjan

Student

TIMETABLE

Semester/Term: _____

Room: _____

Period						
Period						
Period						
Period						
Period						
Period						
Period						
Period						

Copyright © 2001, 2003, 2009 by Stevan Krajnjan

Subject Evaluation Outline

Copyright © 2001, 2003, 2009 by Stevan Krajnjan

SUBJECT:			
Areas Evaluated			

ASSIGNMENTS AND PROJECTS

SUBJECT:			
Description	**Date Assigned**	**%**	**Due Date**

Subject Evaluation Outline

SUBJECT:			

ASSIGNMENTS AND PROJECTS

SUBJECT:			

Copyright © 2001, 2003, 2009 by Stevan Krajnjan

SUBJECT EVALUATION OUTLINE

SUBJECT: _____

Areas of Evaluation			

Copyright © 2001, 2003, 2009 by Stevan Krajnjan

ASSIGNMENTS AND PROJECTS

SUBJECT: _____

Assignment	Start Date	%	Due Date

Class: _____

NAME	FORM	☎		
1.				
2.				
3.				
4.				
5.				
6.				
7.				
8.				
9.				
10.				
11.				
12.				
13.				
14.				
15.				
16.				
17.				
18.				
19.				
20.				
21.				
22.				
23.				
24.				
25.				
26.				
27.				
28.				
29.				
30.				
31.				
32.				
33.				
34.				

Copyright © 2001, 2003, 2009 by Stevan Krajnjan

The Teacher's Binder

Class List

Class: _____

NAME	FORM	☎		
1.				
2.				
3.				
4.				
5.				
6.				
7.				
8.				
9.				
10.				
11.				
12.				
13.				
14.				
15.				
16.				
17.				
18.				
19.				
20.				
21.				
22.				
23.				
24.				
25.				
26.				
27.				
28.				
29.				
30.				
31.				
32.				
33.				
34.				

Copyright © 2001. 2003. 2009 by Stevan Krajnjan

Class List

Class: _____

NAME				
1.				
2.				
3.				
4.				
5.				
6.				
7.				
8.				
9.				
10.				
11.				
12.				
13.				
14.				
15.				
16.				
17.				
18.				
19.				
20.				
21.				
22.				
23.				
24.				
25.				
26.				
27.				
28.				
29.				
30.				
31.				
32.				
33.				
34.				

Copyright © 2001. 2003. 2009 by Stevan Krajnjan

Class List

Room _____

Teacher: _____ Class: _____

Name	☎	Locker Partner	Locker #	Lock Comb.	Lock Serial #

Copyright © 2001. 2003. 2009 by Stevan Krajnjan

Class List

Room: _____

Teacher: _____ Class: _____

Name	☎				

Copyright © 2001, 2003, 2009 by Stevan Krajnjan

The Teacher's Binder

Class List

Teacher: _____ Class: _____

Name	Date of Birth	Home ☎	Work ☎	Cell ☎	E-mail	Emergency Contact

Copyright © 2001, 2003, 2009 by Stevan Krajnjan

SPECIAL  STUDENTS

Student Name   Special Needs

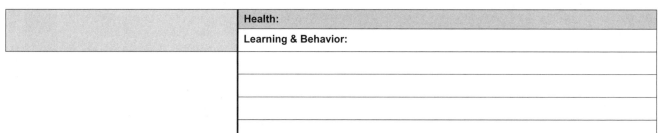

	Health:
	Learning & Behavior:

	Health:
	Learning & Behavior:

	Health:
	Learning & Behavior:

	Health:
	Learning & Behavior:

	Health:
	Learning & Behavior:

Copyright © 2001, 2003, 2009 by Stevan Krajnjan

PARENT/GUARDIAN

IEP Questionnaire

Student: _____

Date: _____

To help develop your child's **Individual Education Plan**, you are invited to answer the following questions. Please return this form to _____ by: _____

1. What is your child able to **do well**, and what are your child's known **strengths** and **abilities?**
_____
_____
_____

2. What in your opinion are **academic** areas in which your child needs to improve? _____
_____
_____
_____
_____

3. Does your child listen to your **directions**, **requests**, and **instructions** at home? _____

4. **What strategy works best** in getting chores or assigned tasks completed at home? _____
_____
_____

5. Does your child **enjoy** going to **school**? Please explain. _____
_____
_____
_____

6. What may be some reasonable **academic goals** for your child to set and achieve this year?
_____
_____
_____

7. How would you ensure that your child has a supportive **study** and **learning environment** at home?
_____
_____

8. What would you like your child to achieve **socially** this year?
_____
_____
_____
_____

9. Are there any **health concerns**, **medications**, or **behaviors** that the teacher should be aware of?
_____
_____
_____

10. **Other** concerns/comments:
_____
_____
_____

Date: _____ Parent/Guardian Signature _____

Copyright © 2001, 2003, 2009 by Stevan Krajnjan

IEP Questionnaire

Student: _____

Date: _____

My **STRENGTHS** ARE:

I find these things **DIFFICULT**:

My **ACADEMIC GOALS** this year are:

My **SOCIAL GOALS** this year are:

To do well in school, I am **PREPARED** to:

Other **CONCERNS/COMMENTS**:

Student Signature: _____ Date: _____

Copyright © 2001, 2003, 2009 by Stevan Krajnjan

Psych Report Summary

STUDENT: _____

Birth Date: _____

Date of Psych Report: _____

School Board of Psych Report: _____

SCORES

Full Scale: _____

Performance Scale: _____

Verbal Scale: _____

ACADEMIC ACHIEVEMENT

Basic Reading: _____

Reading Comp: _____

Listening Comprehension: _____

Spelling: _____

Math Reasoning: _____

Numerical Operations: _____

FORMULATION

OTHER RELEVANT INFORMATION

_____

_____

_____

_____

_____

Copyright © 2001, 2003, 2009 by Stevan Krajnjan

STUDENT INFORMATION SHEET

It is important that our school has the most current administrative information about your child. Please complete this form and return it to your child's teacher **as soon as possible.**

- **STUDENT'S Name:** _____ Class: _____

  Home Address: _____

  Birthday: _____

- **MOTHER'S Name:** _____ Guardian: _____

  Home Telephone: _____ Cell Telephone: _____

  E-mail: _____

  Place of Employment: _____

  Work Telephone: _____ Work E-mail: _____

- **FATHER'S Name:** _____ Guardian: _____

  Home Telephone: _____ Cell Telephone: _____

  E-mail: _____

  Place of Employment: _____

  Work Telephone: _____ Work E-mail: _____

- **EMERGENCY Contact:** _____

  Relationship: _____ Telephone: _____

  Cell Telephone: _____ E-mail: _____

- **Medical Concerns and Information:**

  _____

  _____

  _____

- **Special Needs:**

  _____

  _____

- **Other:** _____

Copyright © 2001, 2003, 2009 by Stevan Krajnjan

STUDENT RECORD SUMMARY

Student: _____ Date of Birth: _____

Teacher: _____ Student Number: _____

- General Background Information:

_____
_____
_____

- School History: _____

- Family: _____
_____

- Health: _____

- **Strengths:**
_____
_____

- **Needs:**
_____
_____
_____
_____
_____

- IEP summary, recommendations:
_____
_____
_____
_____

- **Functioning Levels on (date):** _____

    Reading: _____

    Writing: _____

    Spelling: _____

    Speaking: _____

    Vocabulary: _____

    Math Concepts: _____

    Math Computation: _____

    Math Problem Solving: _____

- Educational Assessment Tool: _____ Date: _____

    Results: _____
_____

Copyright © 2001, 2003, 2009 by Stevan Krajnjan

Student Telephone Directory

Student Name	Phone #	Student Name	Phone #

Copyright © 2001, 2003, 2009 by Stevan Krajnjan

The Teacher's Binder

Student Lockers

Class: _____

Student	Partner	Homeroom	Locker Number	Combination	Serial Number

Copyright © 2001, 2003, 2009 by Stevan Krajnjan

Student Lockers

Class: _____

Student	Locker Number	Combination	Serial Number	

Copyright © 2001, 2003, 2009 by Stevan Krajnjan

The Teacher's Binder

Classroom Procedures

Class **Entry:**
_____
_____
_____
_____

Class **Monitors:**
_____

Classroom **Routines:**
_____
_____
_____
_____
_____
_____
_____

Classroom **Materials:**
_____

Our **Rules** &
Consequences:
_____
_____
_____

LUNCH:
_____
_____

Washrooms Routine:
_____
_____

Dismissal Routine:
_____
_____
_____

Copyright © 2001. 2003. 2009 by Stevan Krajnjan

The Seating Plan

Room: _____

BACK

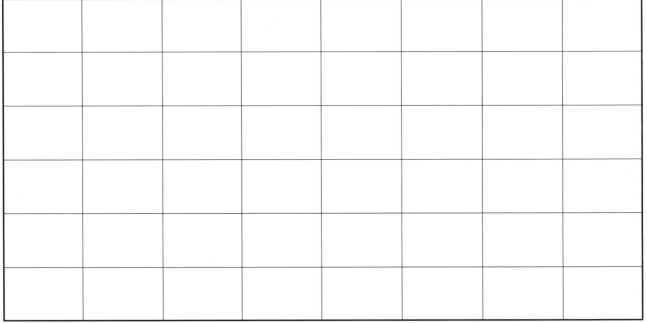

FRONT

Class: _____

BACK

FRONT

Class: _____

Copyright © 2001, 2003, 2009 by Stevan Krajnjan

The Seating Plan

Room: _____

BACK

FRONT

BACK

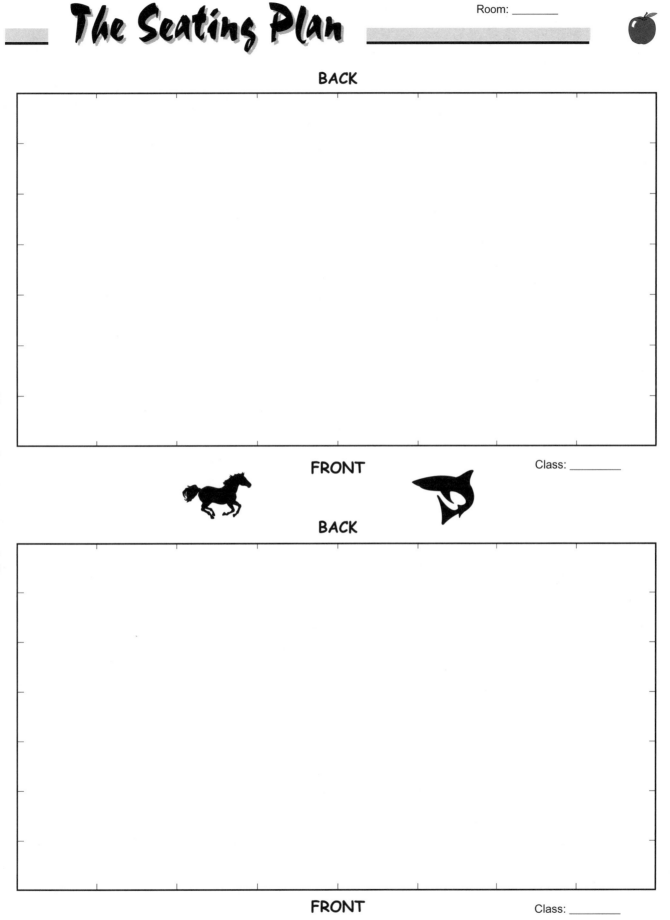

Class: _____

FRONT

Class: _____

Copyright © 2001, 2003, 2009 by Stevan Krajnjan

The Seating Plan

BACK

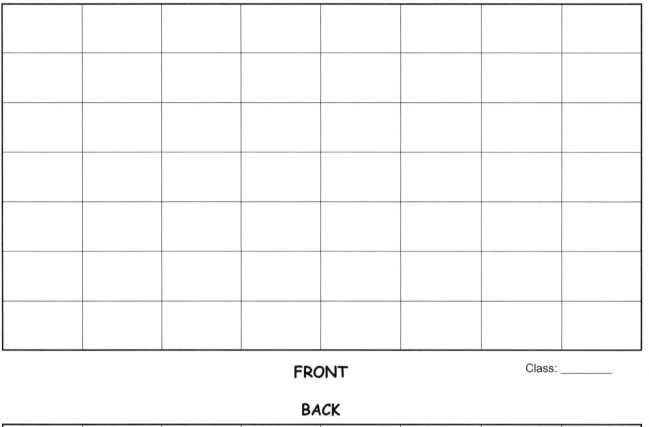

FRONT

Class: _____

BACK

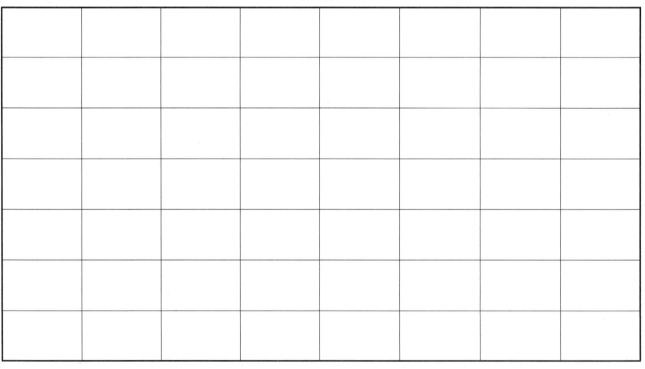

FRONT

Class: _____

Copyright © 2001, 2003, 2009 by Stevan Krajnjan

Teacher: _____ Class: _____ Room: _____

The Seating Plan

BACK OF CLASS

Copyright © 2001, 2003, 2009 by Stevan Krajnjan

FRONT

THE SEATING Plan

Copyright © 2001, 2003, 2009 by Stevan Krajnjan

Class: _____

Blackboard

The Teacher's Binder

Student Profile

Class:_____

Teacher: _____

Room: _____

Student Name	STRENGTHS	NEEDS

Copyright © 2001, 2003, 2009 by Stevan Krajnjan

Class: _____

Teacher: _____

Room: _____

Student Name	STRENGTHS	NEEDS

Copyright © 2001. 2003. 2009 by Stevan Krajnjan

The Teacher's Binder

STUDENT INFORMATION

Name: _____   Date: _____

Teacher: _____   Date of Birth: _____

Background Information:

_____
_____
_____
_____

Family: _____
Health: _____

Strengths:

_____
_____

Needs:

_____
_____
_____
_____
_____

INDIVIDUAL EDUCATION PLAN summary, recommendations:

_____
_____
_____
_____

Student Functioning Levels on (*date*): _____

    LANGUAGE: Listening: _____

                   Speaking: _____

                   Reading: _____

                   Writing: _____

                   Spelling: _____

    MATHEMATICS: Concepts: _____

                       Computation: _____

                       Problem Solving: _____

Educational Assessment Tool/s: _____

Results/Summary: _____
_____

Copyright © 2001, 2003, 2009 by Stevan Krajnjan

Class Integration

Class: _____

Room: _____

Teacher: _____

Student Name	Integrated with	Subject
1.		
2.		
3.		
4.		
5.		
6.		
7.		
8.		
9.		
10.		
11.		
12.		
13.		
14.		
15.		
16.		

Copyright © 2001, 2003, 2009 by Stevan Krajnjan

Name: _____

Class: _____

Date: _____

My Goals!

For This Year

These are the **goals** I aim to achieve **this year**.	This is **how** I plan to do it.
1.	
2.	
3.	
4.	
5.	

Copyright © 2001. 2003. 2009 by Stevan Krajnjan

Setting Goals →

1. _____
2. _____
3. _____

List one to three goals that you plan to achieve. Place a **checkmark** in the appropriate box after you have **achieved** the goal/s for that day. Accomplish your goal/s for **five consecutive** days and receive a reward!

Monday	Tuesday	Wednesday	Thursday	Friday	My Reward!

Copyright © 2001, 2003, 2009 by Stevan Krajnjan

Name: _____

Class: _____

Today's Goal

My **goal** today is: _____

_____

_____

_____

To **succeed** I need to do the following: _____

_____

_____

_____

Copyright © 2001. 2003. 2009 by Stevan Krajnjan

Goal **Achieved!**

✓ ☐

I **have not** achieved my goal.

✓ ☐

My **new goal** is:

_____

_____

_____

My **new strategy** is:

_____

_____

_____

Signature: _____

Date: _____

Witnessed by: _____

✓

MY GOALS FOR THIS WEEK

Name: _____

Class: _____

My **goals** for this week are:

1) _____

2) _____

3) _____

To **succeed** I must do the following: _____

_____

_____

_____

Goals **Achieved!**

✓ ☐

Goals **Not Achieved.**

✓ ☐

My **new goals** are:

1) _____

2) _____

3) _____

My **new strategy** is:

_____

_____

_____

Signature: _____

Date: _____

Witnessed by: _____

Parent's Signature: _____

Copyright © 2001, 2003, 2009 by Stevan Krajnjan

The Teacher's Binder

This is ME!
PERSONAL INVENTORY

My **name is** _____ Some people also call me: _____

My **address** is _____

My home **telephone number** is _____ My **birthday** is on _____

My **family** is made up of _____

I am **interested** in _____

I **do not** like _____

I have a **special friend** whose name is _____

I am very **good at** _____

I am **not** so **good at** _____

I **spend** a lot of time _____

I would **like to learn** about _____

I would be much **better off** if _____

I get really **angry** when _____

I have a few good and bad habits: _____

_____

If I could only **change** the way I _____

Things that I **dislike** in other people: _____

_____

If I was allowed to **help** in class I would _____

This was the **proudest moment** of my life: _____

_____

Some day I will _____

The very **best movie** that I have ever seen: _____

If I could **change** anything, I would first _____

_____

My **feelings about school:** _____

_____

(continued)

Copyright © 2001, 2003, 2009 by Stevan Krajnjan

This is ME!

I often **wish** that _____

_____

I always **learn best** if _____

_____

I find it **difficult** to learn when _____

_____

My biggest role model is _____

If it was possible to **change** one thing about myself it would definitely be _____

If someone could answer wishes, my **three wishes** would be _____

_____

Compared to other families, mine _____

_____

My **accomplishment:** _____

_____

I am very **happy** when _____

The **most important person** in my life is _____

Things that **frustrate** me: _____

_____

I have a **dream**! _____

_____

My **favorite** subjects: _____

The subjects I **don't like:** _____

I **read:**   * rarely * sometimes * often * all the time

When I **look** closely in the mirror, I see _____

_____

There is **something else** I would like to tell you about me: _____

_____

_____

Copyright © 2001, 2003, 2009 by Stevan Krajnjan

Student/Teacher Contract

I, _____, **agree** to perform the following tasks to the best

of my ability: _____

_____

_____

_____

_____

_____

Copyright © 2001, 2003, 2009 by Stevan Krajnjan

_____ guarantees that I will receive the following **privileges/rewards** if

I accomplish the above tasks:

1. _____

2. _____

3. _____

This contract is binding to both parties for the **period** of _____ to _____

This contract will be **REVIEWED** on the following date: _____

Date signed: _____

Student Signature: _____

Teacher Signature: _____

# Student / Teacher Contract

I, _____ , **agree to** perform the following responsibilities

to the best of my ability: _____

_____

_____

_____

_____

_____

_____ **guarantees** that I will receive the following **privileges**

if I successfully complete what I promised:

1. _____

_____

2. _____

_____

3. _____

_____

This contract is **binding** to both parties for the period of _____ to _____

This contract will be **REVIEWED** on the following date: _____

Date signed: _____

Student Signature: _____

Teacher Signature: _____

Copyright © 2001, 2003, 2009 by Stevan Krajnjan

Student/Teacher Contract

I, _____, **agree** to perform the following tasks to the best

of my ability: _____

_____

_____

_____

_____

_____

_____ **guarantees** that I will receive the following **privileges/rewards** if

I accomplish the above tasks:

1. _____

2. _____

3. _____

This contract is binding to both parties for the **period** of _____ to _____

This contract will be **REVIEWED** on the following date: _____

Date signed: _____

Student Signature: _____

Teacher Signature: _____

Copyright © 2001, 2003, 2009 by Stevan Krajnjan

Lesson Plans

Teacher: _____

Week of: _____

	MONDAY	TUESDAY	WEDNESDAY	NOTES
	Date:	Date:	Date:	
Entry Bell				
Period 1	Class: _____	Class: _____	Class: _____	
Period 2	Class: _____	Class: _____	Class: _____	
RECESS				
Period 3	Class: _____	Class: _____	Class: _____	
Period 4	Class: _____	Class: _____	Class: _____	
LUNCH				
Period 5	Class: _____	Class: _____	Class: _____	
Period 6	Class: _____	Class: _____	Class: _____	Photocopy:
Dismissal Bell:				

Copyright © 2001, 2003, 2009 by Stevan Krajnjan

Teacher: _____

Week of: [   ]

ONE WEEK
Lesson Plans

	THURSDAY	FRIDAY	NOTES
	Date:	Date:	
Entry Bell:			
Period **1**	Class: _____	Class: _____	
Period **2**	Class: _____	Class: _____	
RECESS			
Period **3**	Class: _____	Class: _____	
Period **4**	Class: _____	Class: _____	
LUNCH			
Period **5**	Class: _____	Class: _____	
Period **6**	Class: _____	Class: _____	Photocopy:
Dismissal Bell:			

Copyright © 2001. 2003. 2009 by Stevan Krajnjan

The Teacher's Binder

67

ONE WEEK
Lesson Plans

Teacher: _____

Week of: [   ]

	MONDAY	TUESDAY	WEDNESDAY	NOTES
	Date:	Date:	Date:	
Entry Bell				
Period 1	Class: _____	Class: _____	Class: _____	
Period 2	Class: _____	Class: _____	Class: _____	
RECESS				
Period 3	Class: _____	Class: _____	Class: _____	
Period 4	Class: _____	Class: _____	Class: _____	
LUNCH				
Period 5	Class: _____	Class: _____	Class: _____	
Period 6	Class: _____	Class: _____	Class: _____	Photocopy:
Dismissal Bell:				

Copyright © 2001, 2003, 2009 by Stevan Krajnjan

The Teacher's Binder

Teacher: _____

Week of: [   ]

ONE WEEK
Lesson Plans

	THURSDAY	FRIDAY	NOTES
♣	Date:	Date:	✒

Entry Bell: _____

Period 1	Class: _____	Class: _____	
Period 2	Class: _____	Class: _____	
RECESS			
Period 3	Class: _____	Class: _____	
Period 4	Class: _____	Class: _____	
LUNCH			
Period 5	Class: _____	Class: _____	
Period 6	Class: _____	Class: _____	Photocopy:

Dismissal Bell: _____

Copyright © 2001. 2003. 2009 by Stevan Krajnjan

ONE WEEK
Lesson Plans

Teacher: _____

Week of: _____

	MONDAY	TUESDAY	WEDNESDAY	NOTES
	Date:	Date:	Date:	
Entry Bell				
Period 1	Class: _____	Class: _____	Class: _____	
Period 2	Class: _____	Class: _____	Class: _____	
RECESS				
Period 3	Class: _____	Class: _____	Class: _____	
Period 4	Class: _____	Class: _____	Class: _____	
LUNCH				
Period 5	Class: _____	Class: _____	Class: _____	
Period 6	Class: _____	Class: _____	Class: _____	Photocopy:
Dismissal Bell:				

Copyright © 2001, 2003, 2009 by Stevan Krajnjan

The Teacher's Binder

Teacher: _____

Week of: [_____]

ONE WEEK
Lesson Plans

	THURSDAY	FRIDAY	NOTES
✿	Date:	Date:	✒

Entry Bell:

Period **1**	Class: _____	Class: _____	
Period **2**	Class: _____	Class: _____	

RECESS

Period **3**	Class: _____	Class: _____	
Period **4**	Class: _____	Class: _____	

LUNCH

Period **5**	Class: _____	Class: _____	
Period **6**	Class: _____	Class: _____	Photocopy:

Dismissal Bell:

Copyright © 2001. 2003. 2009 by Stevan Krajnjan

The Teacher's Binder

Lesson Plans

Day: _____   **Date:** _____

✎ Reminder!

Per.	Class:	
	Time:	

Per.	Class:	
	Time:	

Per.	Class:	
	Time:	

Per.	Class:	
	Time:	

Per.	Class:	
	Time:	

Per.	Class:	
	Time:	

Per.	Class:	
	Time:	

Per.	Class:	
	Time:	

Photocopy:

Supervision Duties:

Copyright © 2001, 2003, 2009 by Stevan Krajnjan

Lesson Plans

Day: [ ]   **Date:** [ ]

Reminder:

Photocopy:

Supervision Duties:

Copyright © 2001. 2003. 2009 by Stevan Krajnjan

Lesson Plans

Day: _____   **Date:** _____

Reminder:

Per.	Class:	
	Time:	

Per.	Class:	
	Time:	

Per.	Class:	
	Time:	

Per.	Class:	
	Time:	

Lunch ☕

Per.	Class:	
	Time:	

Per.	Class:	
	Time:	

Photocopy:

Supervision Duties:

Copyright © 2001. 2003. 2009 by Stevan Krajnjan

Lesson Plans

Day [ ]   **Date** [ ]

Reminder:

_____: Entry, Lockers, Opening Exercises / **HOMEROOM**

Period	Class:	
1		
Time: —		

Period	Class:	
2		
Time: —		

Period	Class:	
3		
Time: —		

Period	Class:	
4		
Time: —		

_____: **Lunch**

_____: **Entry, Lockers**

LUNCH !

Period	Class:	
5		
Time: —		

Period	Class:	
6		
Time: —		

— Dismissal, Lockers, Remedial, Detention, Extracurricular Activities

Photocopy:

Supervision Duties:

Copyright © 2001, 2003, 2009 by Stevan Krajnjan

Lesson Plans

Day [ ]   **Date** [ ]

Reminder:

_____: Entry, Lockers, Opening Exercises / **HOMEROOM**

Period	Class:	
1		
Time: –		

Period	Class:	
2		
Time: –		

Period	Class:	
3		
Time: –		

_____: **Lunch**

_____: **Entry, Lockers**

LUNCH !

Period	Class:	
4		
Time: –		

Period	Class:	
5		
Time: –		

Period	Class:	
6		
Time: –		

–	Dismissal, Lockers, Remedial, Detention, Extracurricular Activities

Photocopy:

Supervision Duties:

Copyright © 2001. 2003. 2009 by Stevan Krajnjan

DAILY
Lesson Plans

Teacher: _____

Week of:

	MONDAY	TUESDAY	WEDNESDAY	THURSDAY	FRIDAY
Period 1					
Period 2					
Period 3					
LUNCH !					
Period 4					
Period 5					
Period 6					

Dismissal, Lockers, Remedial, Detention, Extracurricular Activities:

Copyright © 2001, 2003, 2009 by Stevan Krajnjan

	MONDAY	TUESDAY	WEDNESDAY	THURSDAY	FRIDAY
Period 1					
Period 2					
Period 3					
Period 4					
LUNCH !					
Period 5					
Period 6					

Dismissal, Lockers, Remedial, Detention, Extracurricular Activities:

Copyright © 2001. 2003. 2009 by Stevan Krajnjan

DAILY
Lesson Plans

Teacher: _____

Week of:

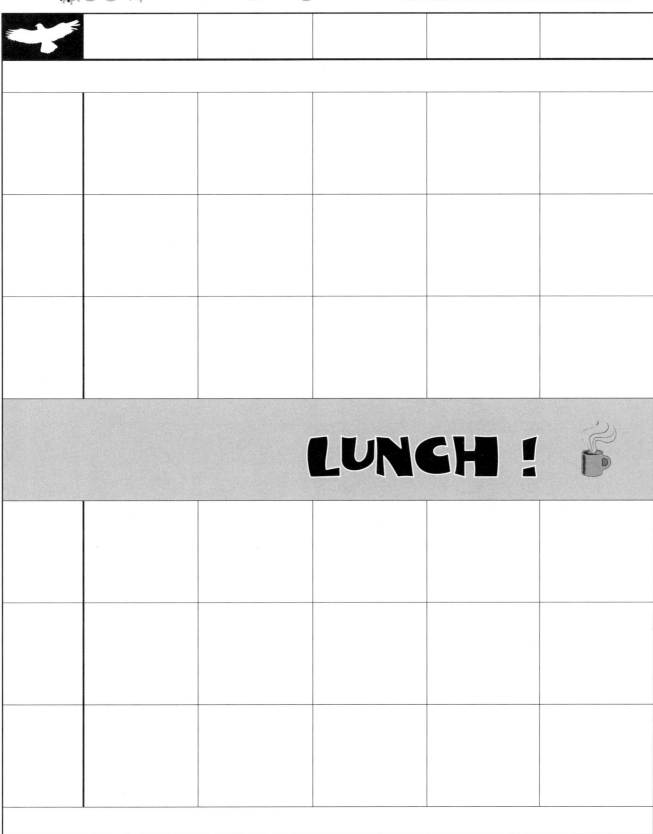

LUNCH !				

Copyright © 2001, 2003, 2009 by Stevan Krajnjan

DAILY Lesson Plans

Teacher: _____

Week of:

LUNCH !					

Dismissal, Lockers, Remedial, Detention, Extracurricular Activities:

Copyright © 2001, 2003, 2009 by Stevan Krajnjan

The Teacher's Binder

Teacher: _____

Week of:

	MONDAY	TUESDAY	WEDNESDAY	THURSDAY	FRIDAY	NOTES
Period 1						
Period 2						
Period 3						
LUNCH !						
Period 4						
Period 5						
Period 6						

Dismissal, Lockers, Remedial, Detention, Extracurricular Activities:

Copyright © 2001, 2003, 2009 by Stevan Krajnjan

DAILY
Lesson Plans

Teacher: _____

Week of:

	MONDAY	TUESDAY	WEDNESDAY	THURSDAY	FRIDAY	NOTES
Period 1						
Period 2						
Period 3						
Period 4						
LUNCH !						
Period 5						
Period 6						

Dismissal, Lockers, Remedial, Detention, Extracurricular Activities:

Copyright © 2001, 2003, 2009 by Stevan Krajnjan

The Teacher's Binder

Lesson Plans

Teacher: _____

Week of:

☀	MONDAY	TUESDAY	WEDNESDAY	THURSDAY	FRIDAY

LUNCH !

Dismissal, Lockers, Remedial, Detention, Extracurricular Activities:

Copyright © 2001, 2003, 2009 by Stevan Krajnjan

DAILY
Lesson Plans

Teacher: _____

Week of:

[   ]

☀	MONDAY	TUESDAY	WEDNESDAY	THURSDAY	FRIDAY
		LUNCH !			

Dismissal, Lockers, Remedial, Detention, Extracurricular Activities:

Copyright © 2001, 2003, 2009 by Stevan Krajnjan

The Teacher's Binder

LESSON PLANS

Week of: _____

	MONDAY	TUESDAY	WEDNESDAY
TIME:			
TIME:			
LUNCH			
TIME:			
TIME:			

Photocopy:

Supervision Duties:

Copyright © 2001, 2003, 2009 by Stevan Krajnjan

	THURSDAY	FRIDAY	Notes
TIME:			
TIME:			
🌼	**LUNCH**		
TIME:			
TIME:			
✒			

Photocopy:

Supervision Duties:

Copyright © 2001, 2003, 2009 by Stevan Krajnjan

LESSON PLANS

Week of:

	MONDAY	TUESDAY	WEDNESDAY

LUNCH

Photocopy:

Supervision Duties:

Copyright © 2001, 2003, 2009 by Stevan Krajnjan

	THURSDAY	FRIDAY	Notes

LUNCH

Photocopy:

Supervision Duties:

Copyright © 2001, 2003, 2009 by Stevan Krajnjan

Single Lesson Plan

Date: _____ Period: _____

LESSON TITLE: _____

SUBJECT: _____ Level/Grade: _____ **Length:** _____

GENERAL EXPECTATIONS: _____

SPECIFIC EXPECTATIONS: _____

LESSON PLAN STEPS:

Introduction: _____

1. _____
2. _____
3. _____
4. _____
5. _____
6. _____
7. _____
8. _____

Conclusion: _____
_____

ASSIGNMENT: _____

MATERIALS: _____
_____
_____

AUDIO-VISUAL: _____

ENRICHMENT / EXTENSION: _____
_____

ASSESSMENT: _____

PHOTOCOPY: _____

MANAGEMENT & NOTES: _____
_____
_____
_____

Copyright © 2001, 2003, 2009 by Stevan Krajnjan

SINGLE SUBJECT

Weekly Lesson Plans

Teacher: _____

WEEK OF: _____

MONDAY

DATE:

Day:

Classes:

LESSON:

Objective:

Materials & Resources:

Photocopy:

Supervision Duties

TUESDAY

DATE:

Day:

Classes:

LESSON:

Objective:

Materials & Resources:

Photocopy:

Supervision Duties

WEDNESDAY

DATE:

Day:

Classes:

LESSON:

Objective:

Materials & Resources:

Photocopy:

Supervision Duties

THURSDAY

DATE:

Day:

Classes:

LESSON:

Objective:

Materials & Resources:

Photocopy:

Supervision Duties

FRIDAY

DATE:

Day:

Classes:

LESSON:

Objective:

Materials & Resources:

Photocopy:

Supervision Duties

Copyright © 2001, 2003, 2009 by Stevan Krajnjan

The Teacher's Binder

STAFF MEETINGS

Date	Agenda & Notes
Reminder:	

Copyright © 2001, 2003, 2009 by Stevan Krajnjan

STAFF MEETINGS

Date	Agenda & Notes

Reminder:

Copyright © 2001. 2003. 2009 by Stevan Krajnjan

The Teacher's Binder

STAFF MEETINGS

Date	Meeting Notes
	🏳 Important!

Date	Meeting Notes
	🏳 Important!

Date	Meeting Notes
	🏳 Important!

Additional Notes:

Copyright © 2001, 2003, 2009 by Stevan Krajnjan

Student Anecdotals

Student: _____

DATE	NOTES AND OBSERVATIONS

Copyright © 2001, 2003, 2009 by Stevan Krajnjan

Student Behavior Log

Student: _____

DATE	NOTES AND OBSERVATIONS

Copyright © 2001, 2003, 2009 by Stevan Krajnjan

ASSIGNMENT OR HOMEWORK

Monitor Sheet

Student: _____
Teacher: _____
Homeroom: _____

Date	Assignment or Homework	Teacher Signature	Parent Signature	✓ Done

Copyright © 2001, 2003, 2009 by Stevan Krajnjan

The Teacher's Binder

ASSIGNMENT OR HOMEWORK

Monitor Sheet

Student: _____

Teacher: _____

Homeroom: _____

Date	Assignment or Homework	Teacher	Parent	✓

Copyright © 2001. 2003. 2009 by Stevan Krajnjan

School Supplies

CHECKLIST

Bring the following **school supplies** with you to class every day:

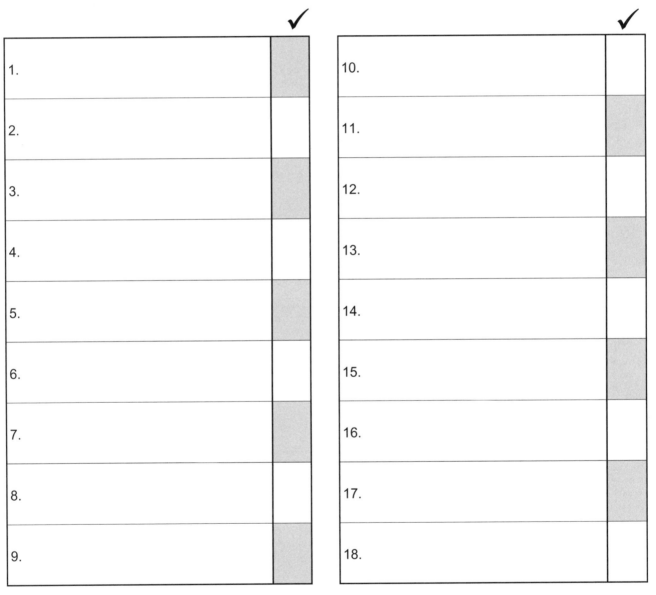

✓		✓
1.		10.
2.		11.
3.		12.
4.		13.
5.		14.
6.		15.
7.		16.
8.		17.
9.		18.

19. Great Attitude! ✓

Copyright © 2001, 2003, 2009 by Stevan Krajnjan

HOMEWORK NOT DONE

Just a brief note to inform you that _____ has not completed the following homework:

Subject:	
Assigned on:	
Due on:	

Homework:

Teacher:

Parent Signature: _____ Date: _____

HOMEWORK NOT DONE !

Just a brief note to inform you that _____ has not completed the following homework:

Subject:	
Assigned on:	
Due on:	

Homework:

Teacher:

Parent Signature: _____ Date: _____

Copyright © 2001, 2003, 2009 by Stevan Krajnjan

Homework Not Done

This note is to inform you that _____

has not completed the following homework assignment:

Subject: _____

Date Assigned: _____

Date Due: _____

Details: _____

_____

_____

Teacher: _____ Date: _____

Parent/Guardian Signature: _____

Copyright © 2001, 2003, 2009 by Stevan Krajnjan

Homework Not Done

This note is to inform you that _____

has not completed the following homework assignment:

Subject: _____

Date Assigned: _____

Date Due: _____

Details: _____

_____

_____

Teacher: _____ Date: _____

Parent/Guardian Signature: _____

✂ -

ASSIGNMENT NOT DONE

Just a brief note to inform you that _____ has not completed the following assignment:

Subject:	
Assigned on:	
Due on:	

Assignment:

Teacher:

Parent Signature: _____ Date: _____

✂ - ✂

Copyright © 2001, 2003, 2009 by Stevan Krajnjan

✂ -

Assignment Not Done!

Just a brief note to inform you that _____ has not completed the following assignment:

Subject:	
Assigned on:	
Due on:	

Assignment:

Teacher:

Parent Signature: _____ Date: _____

✂ - ✂

Missing Assignment

This note is to inform you that _____

has not completed the following assignment:

Subject: _____

Date Assigned: _____

Date Due: _____

Details: _____

_____

_____

Teacher: _____ Date: _____

Parent/Guardian Signature: _____

Copyright © 2001, 2003, 2009 by Stevan Krajnjan

Missing Assignment

This note is to inform you that _____

has not completed the following assignment:

Subject: _____

Date Assigned: _____

Date Due: _____

Details: _____

_____

_____

Teacher: _____ Date: _____

Parent/Guardian Signature: _____

✂ -

REMINDER !

Just a brief note to inform you that _____ has **not** completed the following work:

Subject:	
Assigned on:	
Due on:	

Assigned Work:

Teacher:

Parent Signature: _____ Date: _____

Copyright © 2001, 2003, 2009 by Stevan Krajnjan

✂ -

REMINDER !

Just a brief note to inform you that _____ has not completed the following work:

Subject:	
Assigned on:	
Due on:	

Assigned Work:

Teacher:

Parent Signature: _____ Date: _____

Homework Record

Class: _____

Student Name										

Copyright © 2001. 2003. 2009 by Stevan Krajnjan

Class: _____

Student Name	Homework:												

Copyright © 2001. 2003. 2009 by Stevan Krajnjan

Homework Excuse Note

Have students fill out a HOMEWORK EXCUSE NOTE every time assigned work is overdue or not completed. Share the saved notes with parents/guardians during an interview if homework completion becomes a problem. This strategy may help improve student work habits.

HOMEWORK EXCUSE NOTE

I did not complete _____

_____

(assigned homework/assignment)

for the following reason: _____

_____

_____

_____

_____ Date: _____
Signature

HOMEWORK EXCUSE NOTE

I did not complete _____

_____

(assigned homework/assignment)

for the following reason: _____

_____

_____

_____

_____ Date: _____
Signature

HOMEWORK EXCUSE NOTE

I did not complete _____

_____

(assigned homework/assignment)

for the following reason: _____

_____

_____

_____

_____ Date: _____
Signature

HOMEWORK EXCUSE NOTE

I did not complete _____

_____

(assigned homework/assignment)

for the following reason: _____

_____

_____

_____

_____ Date: _____
Signature

Copyright © 2001. 2003. 2009 by Stevan Krajnjan

What We Did in Class

Teacher: _____

Year: _____

	Subject	Subject	Subject
SEPTEMBER			
OCTOBER			
NOVEMBER			
DECEMBER			
JANUARY			

Copyright © 2001, 2003, 2009 by Stevan Krajnjan

WHAT WE DID IN CLASS

Teacher: _____

Year: _____

	Subject	Subject	Subject
FEBRUARY			
MARCH			
APRIL			
MAY			
JUNE			

Copyright © 2001. 2003. 2009 by Stevan Krajnjan

The Teacher's Binder

PARENT - TEACHER CONFERENCE NOTICE

Dear Parent/Guardian of _____:

A parent-teacher conference has been scheduled for you with _____ on

Date: _____ **Time:** _____ **Room:** _____.

Please complete this form below and return it by: _____

I am **able** to attend _____. I am **unable** to attend _____. ✓

Please **reschedule** the conference for _____ or _____.

_____   _____   _____
             Signature   Telephone Number   E-mail

✂ -

PARENT - TEACHER CONFERENCE NOTICE

Dear Parent/Guardian of _____:

A parent-teacher conference has been scheduled for you with _____ on

Date: _____ **Time:** _____ **Room:** _____.

Please complete this form below and return it by: _____

I am **able** to attend _____. I am **unable** to attend _____. ✓

Please **reschedule** the conference for _____ or _____.

_____   _____   _____
             Signature   Telephone Number   E-mail

Copyright © 2001, 2003, 2009 by Stevan Krajnjan

PARENT-TEACHER INTERVIEW NOTICE

Dear Parent/Guardian of _____:

A parent-teacher interview has been scheduled for you with _____ on

Date: _____ **Time:** _____ **Room:** _____.

Please complete this form below and return it by: _____

I am **able** to attend _____.   I am **unable** to attend _____.   ✓

Please **reschedule** the interview for _____ or _____.

_____   _____   _____
Signature   Telephone Number   E-mail

✂ -

Parent - Teacher Interview NOTICE

Dear Parent/Guardian of _____:

A parent-teacher interview has been scheduled for you with _____ on

Date: _____ **Time:** _____ **Room:** _____.

Please complete this form below and return it by: _____

I am **able** to attend _____.   I am **unable** to attend _____.   ✓

Please **reschedule** the conference for _____ or _____.

_____   _____   _____
Signature   Telephone Number   E-mail

Copyright © 2001, 2003, 2009 by Stevan Krajnjan

Interview Schedule

TEACHER: _____ Date: _____ Room: _____

TIME	NAME OF PARENT/GUARDIAN
3:15	
3:30	
3:45	
4:00	
4:15	
4:30	
4:45	
5:00	
5:15	
5:30	
5:45	
6:00	
6:15	
6:30	
6:45	
7:00	
7:15	
7:30	
7:45	
8:00	
8:15	
8:30	
8:45	

Copyright © 2001, 2003, 2009 by Stevan Krajnjan

Interview Schedule

TEACHER: _____ Date: _____ Room: _____

TIME	NAME OF PARENT/GUARDIAN

Copyright © 2001, 2003, 2009 by Stevan Krajnjan

The Teacher's Binder

Interview Schedule

TEACHER: _____ Date: _____ Room: _____

TIME	PARENT/GUARDIAN
8:30	
8:45	
9:00	
9:15	
10:00	
10:15	
10:30	
10:45	
11:00	
11:15	
11:30	
11:45	
12:00	
12:15	
12:30	
12:45	
1:00	
1:15	
1:30	
1:45	
2:00	
2:15	
2:30	

TIME	PARENT/GUARDIAN
3:15	
3:30	
3:45	
4:00	
4:15	
4:30	
4:45	
5:00	
5:15	
5:30	
5:45	
6:00	
6:15	
6:30	
6:45	
7:00	
7:15	
7:30	
7:45	
8:00	
8:15	
8:30	
8:45	

Copyright © 2001. 2003. 2009 by Stevan Krajnjan

Interview Schedule

🍎

TEACHER: _____   Room: _____

DATE: _____

TIME	PARENT/GUARDIAN
8:30	
8:45	
9:00	
9:15	
10:00	
10:15	
10:30	
10:45	
11:00	
11:15	
11:30	
11:45	
12:00	
12:15	
12:30	
12:45	
1:00	
1:15	
1:30	
1:45	
2:00	
2:15	
2:30	

DATE: _____

TIME	PARENT/GUARDIAN
3:15	
3:30	
3:45	
4:00	
4:15	
4:30	
4:45	
5:00	
5:15	
5:30	
5:45	
6:00	
6:15	
6:30	
6:45	
7:00	
7:15	
7:30	
7:45	
8:00	
8:15	
8:30	
8:45	

Copyright © 2001, 2003, 2009 by Stevan Krajnjan

The Teacher's Binder

INTERVIEW SCHEDULE

TEACHER: _____   Room: _____

DATE: _____   DATE: _____

TIME	PARENT/GUARDIAN

TIME	PARENT/GUARDIAN

Copyright © 2001, 2003, 2009 by Stevan Krajnjan

PARENT/TEACHER CONFERENCE

PREPARATION Sheet

Interview Date: _____

Student Name	Doing Well in	Areas of Concern	Notes
Interview Time: _____			
Interview Time: _____			
Interview Time: _____			
Interview Time: _____			
Interview Time: _____			
Interview Time: _____			

Copyright © 2001, 2003, 2009 by Stevan Krajnjan

Parent Interview PREPARATION Sheet

STUDENT: _____ Class: _____ Interview Date: _____ Time: _____

Doing Well in:	Areas of Concern	Next Steps	Other Information

Notes: _____
_____
_____
_____
_____
_____

Copyright © 2001, 2003, 2009 by Stevan Krajnjan

✂ -

Parent Interview PREPARATION Sheet

STUDENT: _____ Class: _____ Interview Date: _____ Time: _____

Doing Well in:	Areas of Concern	Next Steps	Other Information

Notes: _____
_____
_____
_____
_____
_____

Parent/Teacher Conference PREPARATION Sheet

STUDENT: _____ Class: _____ Interview Date: _____ Time: _____

Doing Well in:	Areas of Concern	Next Steps	Other Information

Notes:

Parent/Teacher Conference PREPARATION Sheet

STUDENT: _____ Class: _____ Interview Date: _____ Time: _____

Doing Well in:	Areas of Concern	Next Steps	Other Information

Notes:

Copyright © 2001, 2003, 2009 by Stevan Krajnjan

The Teacher's Binder

PARENT CONFERENCES RECORD SHEET

Name of Parent	DATE	Comments

Copyright © 2001. 2003. 2009 by Stevan Krajnjan

PARENT CONFERENCE RECORD SHEET

Student Name:	Comments:
Conference Date:	
Parent:	
Follow-up:	

Student Name:	Comments:
Conference Date:	
Parent:	
Follow-up:	

Student Name:	Comments:
Conference Date:	
Parent:	
Follow-up:	

Copyright © 2001. 2003. 2009 by Stevan Krajnjan

The Teacher's Binder

Teacher: _____

Parent Contact

Parent	DATE	Comments

Copyright © 2001, 2003, 2009 by Stevan Krajnjan

Parent Contact

Date	Parent Name	Subject of Discussion	Notes

Copyright © 2001, 2003, 2009 by Stevan Krajnjan

PARENT CONTACT

Date	NAME	COMMENT

Copyright © 2001. 2003. 2009 by Stevan Krajnjan

Year _____

Diagnostic Testing RECORD

Student Name	Area of Testing: Type of Test: Date:	Area of Testing: Type of Test: Date:	Area of Testing: Type of Test: Date:	Area of Testing: Type of Test: Date:	Area of Testing: Type of Test: Date:	Area of Testing: Type of Test: Date:
1.						
2.						
3.						
4.						
5.						
6.						
7.						
8.						
9.						
10.						
11.						
12.						
13.						
14.						
15.						
16.						

Copyright © 2001, 2003, 2009 by Stevan Krajnjan

Academic Year:

_____

Diagnostic Testing RECORD

Student:	Area of Testing: Type of Test: Date:	Area of Testing: Type of Test: Date:	Area of Testing: Type of Test: Date:	Area of Testing: Type of Test: Date:	Area of Testing: Type of Test: Date:	Area of Testing: Type of Test: Date:
1.						
2.						
3.						
4.						
5.						
6.						
7.						
8.						
9.						
10.						
11.						
12.						
13.						
14.						
15.						

Copyright © 2001, 2003, 2009 by Stevan Krajnjan

STUDENT
Functioning Levels

Date: _____

Class: _____

Student Name	Reading	Writing	Spelling	Oral Communication	Listening	Math Concepts	Math Problem Solving	Math Computation

Copyright © 2001, 2003, 2009 by Stevan Krajnjan

The Teacher's Binder

Writing Achievement Levels

Date _____

Class _____

Copyright © 2001, 2003, 2009 by Stevan Krajnjan

Student Name	CONTENT ◆ Is the main idea clear? ◆ Stays on topic? ◆ Is content interesting, original, thoughtful? ◆ Is there evidence of supporting details? ◆ Does the writing make sense?	ORGANIZATION ◆ Are introduction and conclusion effective? ◆ Is there evidence of plan and sequencing? ◆ Are linking words used? ◆ Are paragraphs used?	CONVENTIONS ◆ Spelling ◆ Punctuation ◆ Grammar ◆ Do errors get in way of understanding the message? ◆ Are revision and corrections needed?	VOICE ◆ Is reader's attention captured? ◆ Does the writing sound sincere and convincing? ◆ Does the reader get emotionally involved?	USE OF LANGUAGE ◆ Are the words used descriptive, imaginative, and effective? ◆ Are variety of words used? ◆ Are literary devices used?

WRITING ACHIEVEMENT LEVELS

Date _____

Class _____

Student Name	HANDWRITING ◆ Is the written text easy to read? ◆ Does the writing meet the grade-level expectations?	SPELLING & PUNCTUATION ◆ Are there many spelling errors? ◆ Are there many punctuation errors?	SENTENCE STRUCTURE ◆ Are the sentences gram-matically correct? ◆ Is there a subject/verb agreement?	PARAGRAPHS ◆ Are paragraphs used? ◆ Are sentences on the same topic? ◆ Do sentences flow through the use of linking words?	STORY CONSTRUCTION ◆ Are the begin-ning, middle, and end in correct order? ◆ Does the story flow between paragraphs? ◆ Do all para-graphs tell one story—one topic?

Copyright © 2001. 2003. 2009 by Stevan Krajnjan

The Teacher's Binder

Date _____

Class _____

Copyright © 2001, 2003, 2009 by Stevan Krajnjan

Student Name	LANGUAGE CONVENTIONS ◆ Does the student understand and use text conventions (spelling, grammar, punctuation, and style) during reading? ◆ Is the student able to identify spelling, punctuation, and style conventions, and explain how they are used during reading?	READING STRATEGIES ◆ Are strategies used to decode unfamiliar words? ◆ Is the student able to read prefixes, suffixes, patterns? ◆ Are cueing systems used to assist with reading? ◆ Is there evidence of self-correction for meaning?	COMMUNICATION ◆ Is the student able to retell accurately? ◆ Is the student able to make connections to personal experiences and knowledge? ◆ Is the student able to predict, infer, and justify? ◆ Is the student able to point out cause and effect?	PRINT & TEXT FEATURES ◆ Is the student able to read different text and print formats? ◆ Are various forms of writing understood? ◆ Is there evidence of ability to use non-print information (graphs, photos, drawings, etc.) for meaning?

Personal Home Reading Log

Dear Parents/Guardians:

Decoding and reading comprehension skills can improve through **regular**, consistent, and meaningful **daily reading**. **Personal Home Reading Log** is designed to keep track of what, how often, and how long your child reads at home. Please help monitor your child's reading activities by signing the Log. By doing so you are confirming that the required reading has taken place. Students are encouraged to select reading material from the genre of their choice and read at least 20 minutes every day. Please return the signed sheet on _____.

NAME: _____ Reading period **beginning**: _____ and **ending**: _____

Date	What I read	Number of pages	Number of minutes I spent reading	Student Signature	Parent Signature

Copyright © 2001. 2003. 2009 by Stevan Krajnjan

The Teacher's Binder

PERSONAL HOME READING LOG

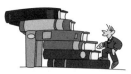

Dear Parents/Guardians:

Decoding and reading comprehension skills can improve through **regular**, consistent, and meaningful **daily reading**. **Personal Home Reading Log** is designed to keep track of what, how often, and how long your child reads at home. Please help monitor your child's reading activities by signing the Log. By doing so you are confirming that the required reading has taken place. Students are encouraged to select reading material from the genre of their choice and read at least 20 minutes every day. Please return the signed sheet on _____.

NAME: _____ Reading period **beginning**: _____ and **ending**: _____

Date	What I read	Number of pages	Number of minutes I spent reading	Student Signature	Parent Signature

Copyright © 2001, 2003, 2009 by Stevan Krajnjan

Use as a bookmark

BOOKMARK

NAME: _____

Reading Log Due Date: _____

Parent Signature: _____

Date	Book Title	Pages Read	Parent Initial

Use as a bookmark

BOOKMARK

NAME: _____

Reading Log Due Date: _____

Parent Signature: _____

Date	What I read	Pages Read	Parent Initial

Copyright © 2001, 2003, 2009 by Stevan Krajnjan

Copyright © 2001. 2003. 2009 by Stevan Krajnjan

Use as a bookmark

BOOK JOT NOTES

BOOK TITLE: _____

_____

Start Date: _____

End Date: _____

Words to Look Up:

_____

_____

_____

_____

_____

_____

_____

_____

_____

Notes:

_____

_____

_____

Use as a bookmark

Book Jot Notes

BOOK TITLE: _____

_____

Start Date: _____

End Date: _____

Words to Look Up:

_____

_____

_____

_____

_____

_____

_____

_____

Notes:

_____

_____

_____

BOOK JOT NOTES

Use as a bookmark

BOOK TITLE: _____

_____

Start Date: _____

End Date: _____

Words to Look Up:

_____

_____

_____

_____

_____

_____

_____

_____

_____

Notes:

Character Names:

_____

_____

_____

_____

BOOK JOT NOTES

Use as a bookmark

BOOK TITLE: _____

_____

Start Date: _____

End Date: _____

Words to Look Up:

_____

_____

_____

_____

_____

_____

_____

_____

_____

Notes:

Character Names:

_____

_____

_____

_____

Copyright © 2001, 2003, 2009 by Stevan Krajnjan

Year: _____

Subject: _____

Teacher: _____

Student Name	TERM 1						Report Card Mark	TERM 2						Report Card Mark	TERM 3						Report Card Mark

Copyright © 2001. 2003. 2009 by Stevan Krajnjan

Subject: _____

Teacher: _____

School Year: _____

Copyright © 2001, 2003, 2009 by Stevan Krajnjan

Student Name	TERM 1						Report Card Mark	TERM 2						Report Card Mark	TERM 3						Report Card Mark

Subject: _____

Copyright © 2001, 2003, 2009 by Stevan Krajnjan

Teacher: _____

School Year: _____

From: _____ to: _____

Student Name	TERM _____																		Report Card Mark

Subject: _____

Teacher: _____

School Year: _____

	From: ____ to: ____						From: ____ to: ____						From: ____ to: ____					
Student Name	SEMESTER 1					Report Card Mark	SEMESTER 2					Report Card Mark	SEMESTER 3					Report Card Mark

Copyright © 2001, 2003, 2009 by Stevan Krajnjan

Reading

Teacher: _____
School Year: _____

| From: _____ to: _____ | From: _____ to: _____ | From: _____ to: _____ |

Student Name	TERM 1						Report Card Mark	TERM 2						Report Card Mark	TERM 3						Report Card Mark

Copyright © 2001, 2003, 2009 by Stevan Krajnjan

Writing

Teacher: _____

School Year: _____

	From: _____ to: _____					From: _____ to: _____					From: _____ to: _____				
	TERM 1					TERM 2					TERM 3				
Student Name						Report Card Mark						Report Card Mark					Report Card Mark

Copyright © 2001, 2003, 2009 by Stevan Krajnjan

The Teacher's Binder

Oral and Visual Communication

Teacher: _____

School Year: _____

From: _____ to: _____   From: _____ to: _____   From: _____ to: _____

Student Name	TERM 1						Report Card Mark	TERM 2						Report Card Mark	TERM 3						Report Card Mark

Copyright © 2001, 2003, 2009 by Stevan Krajnjan

Number Sense and Numeration

Teacher: _____

School Year: _____

| From: _____ to: _____ | From: _____ to: _____ | From: _____ to: _____ |

Student Name	TERM 1						Report Card Mark	TERM 2						Report Card Mark	TERM 3						Report Card Mark

Copyright © 2001, 2003, 2009 by Stevan Krajnjan

Measurement

Teacher: _____

School Year: _____

From: _____ to: _____	From: _____ to: _____	From: _____ to: _____

Student Name	TERM 1					Report Card Mark	TERM 2					Report Card Mark	TERM 3					Report Card Mark

Copyright © 2001, 2003, 2009 by Stevan Krajnjan

Geometry and Spatial Sense

Copyright © 2001, 2003, 2009 by Stevan Krajnjan

Teacher: _____

School Year: _____

From: _____ to: _____   From: _____ to: _____   From: _____ to: _____

Student Name	TERM 1						Report Card Mark	TERM 2						Report Card Mark	TERM 3						Report Card Mark

Data Management and Probability

Teacher: _____

School Year: _____

From: _____ to: _____   From: _____ to: _____   From: _____ to: _____

Student Name	TERM 1						Report Card Mark	TERM 2						Report Card Mark	TERM 3						Report Card Mark

Copyright © 2001, 2003, 2009 by Stevan Krajnjan

Patterning and Algebra

Teacher: _____

School Year: _____

From: _____ to: _____   From: _____ to: _____   From: _____ to: _____

Student Name	TERM 1						Report Card Mark	TERM 2						Report Card Mark	TERM 3						Report Card Mark

Copyright © 2001, 2003, 2009 by Stevan Krajnjan

The Teacher's Binder

Science and Technology

Copyright © 2001, 2003, 2009 by Stevan Krajnjan

Marks

Teacher: _____

School Year: _____

From: _____ to: _____   From: _____ to: _____   From: _____ to: _____

Student Name	TERM 1						Report Card Mark	TERM 2						Report Card Mark	TERM 3						Report Card Mark

History

Teacher: _____

School Year: _____

From: _____ to: _____   From: _____ to: _____   From: _____ to: _____

Student Name	TERM 1						Report Card Mark	TERM 2						Report Card Mark	TERM 3						Report Card Mark

Copyright © 2001, 2003, 2009 by Stevan Krajnjan

The Teacher's Binder

Marks

Geography

Teacher: _____

School Year: _____

Student Name	TERM 1						Report Card Mark	TERM 2						Report Card Mark	TERM 3						Report Card Mark

Copyright © 2001, 2003, 2009 by Stevan Krajnjan

Music

Teacher: _____

School Year: _____

From: _____ to: _____   From: _____ to: _____   From: _____ to: _____

Student Name	TERM 1						Report Card Mark	TERM 2						Report Card Mark	TERM 3						Report Card Mark

Copyright © 2001, 2003, 2009 by Stevan Krajnjan

The Teacher's Binder

Art

Marks

Teacher: _____

School Year: _____

From: _____ to: _____	From: _____ to: _____	From: _____ to: _____

Student Name	TERM 1						Report Card Mark	TERM 2						Report Card Mark	TERM 3						Report Card Mark

Copyright © 2001, 2003, 2009 by Stevan Krajnjan

Physical and Health Education

Teacher: _____

School Year: _____

From: _____ to: _____   From: _____ to: _____   From: _____ to: _____

Student Name	TERM 1							Report Card Mark	TERM 2							Report Card Mark	TERM 3							Report Card Mark

Copyright © 2001, 2003, 2009 by Stevan Krajnjan

Marks

French

Copyright © 2001, 2003, 2009 by Stevan Krajnjan

Teacher: _____

School Year: _____

From: _____ to: _____   From: _____ to: _____   From: _____ to: _____

Student Name	TERM 1						Report Card Mark	TERM 2						Report Card Mark	TERM 3						Report Card Mark

French MODIFIED PROGRAM

Teacher: _____

School Year: _____

From: _____ to: _____

Student Name	READING						Report Card Mark	WRITING					Report Card Mark	ORAL					Report Card Mark

Copyright © 2001, 2003, 2009 by Stevan Krajnjan

Evaluation

Subject: _____

Class: _____

Date ➜

Student

FINAL MARK

	Student											FINAL MARK	
1													1
2													2
3													3
4													4
5													5
6													6
7													7
8													8
9													9
10													10
11													11
12													12
13													13
14													14
15													15
16													16
17													17
18													18
19													19
20													20
21													21
22													22
23													23
24													24
25													25
26													26
27													27
28													28
29													29
30													30

Copyright © 2001, 2003, 2009 by Stevan Krajnjan

Class: _____

Use of Student Planner

X - not brought to class   **N** - not used as instructed   ✓ – used as instructed

Student Name				DATE																

Copyright © 2001, 2003, 2009 by Stevan Krajnjan

Class: _____

 # Use of Student Organizer

X - not brought to class   **N** - not used as instructed   ✓ – used as instructed

Student Name	DATE																				

Copyright © 2001, 2003, 2009 by Stevan Krajnjan

Class: _____

X - not brought to class   N - not used as instructed   ✓ – used as instructed

Student Name	DATE																					

Copyright © 2001, 2003, 2009 by Stevan Krajnjan

Class: _____

Use of Student Agenda

X - not brought to class   **N** - not used as instructed   ✓ – used as instructed

Student Name	DATE																				

Copyright © 2001, 2003, 2009 by Stevan Krajnjan

Assignment Record

NAME									
1.									
2.									
3.									
4.									
5.									
6.									
7.									
8.									
9.									
10.									
11.									
12.									
13.									
14.									
15.									
16.									

Copyright © 2001, 2003, 2009 by Stevan Krajnjan

Peer Evaluation

Student Evaluated:	Title:

What was done well:

Areas that need improvement:

Evaluator:

✂ --

Student Evaluated:	Title:

What was done well:

Areas that need improvement:

Evaluator:

Copyright © 2001, 2003, 2009 by Stevan Krajnjan

Peer Editing Form

Ask a **classmate** to read through what you have written, check off the box next to each question, and write a brief comment that will help improve your work. Underlining and changes are permitted if done in **pencil**.

Peer Editor: _____   **Date**: _____

Author: _____   **Work Title**: _____

	Yes	No	Comment
1. Is there evidence of **prewriting** (brainstorming, planning)?			
2. Are the **title** main words **capitalized**?			
3. Does the **title fit** the work?			
4. Are **paragraphs used** to organize information?			
5. Is the **introduction** effective?			
6. Is the **main idea** clear, with a **sense of purpose**?			
7. Is information placed in **logical order**?			
8. Is there enough **supporting evidence**?			
9. Does the writer stay **on topic**?			
10. Is the writing **interesting**?			
11. Is the **word choice** appropriate?			
12. Does each **sentence begin** with a **capital letter**?			
13. Does each **sentence end** with proper **punctuation**?			
14. Is each **sentence** a **complete thought**?			
15. Are there any **spelling errors** (*underline please*)?			
16. Are there other words that should be **capitalized**?			
17. Are **plurals** and **possessives** correct?			
18. Are **quotation marks** used correctly?			
19. Is the **conclusion** effective and relevant?			
20. Is **written text** well **organized** on paper?			

Other comments:

Copyright © 2001, 2003, 2009 by Stevan Krajnjan

Peer Editing Form

Ask a **classmate** to read through what you have written, check off the box next to each question, and write a brief comment that will help improve your work. Underlining and changes are permitted if done in **pencil**.

Peer Editor: _____ Date: _____

Author: _____ Work Title: _____

	Yes	No	Comment
1. Is there evidence of **prewriting** (brainstorming, planning)?			
2. Are the **title** main words **capitalized**?			
3. Does the **title fit** the work?			
4. Are **paragraphs used** to organize information?			
5. Is the **introduction** effective?			
6. Is the **main idea** clear, with a **sense of purpose**?			
7. Is information placed in **logical order**?			
8. Is there enough **supporting evidence**?			
9. Does the writer stay **on topic**?			
10. Is the writing **interesting**?			
11. Is the **word choice** appropriate?			
12. Does each **sentence begin** with **capital letter**?			
13. Does each **sentence end** with proper **punctuation**?			
14. Is each **sentence a complete thought**?			
15. Are there any **spelling errors** (**underline please**)?			
16. Are there other words that should be **capitalized**?			
17. Are **plurals** and **possessives** correct?			
18. Are **quotation marks** used correctly?			
19. Is the **conclusion** effective and relevant?			
20. Is **written text** well **organized** on paper?			
Other Comments			

Peer Editing Form

Ask a **classmate** to read through what you have written, check off the box next to each question, and write a brief comment that will help improve your work. Underlining and changes are permitted if done in **pencil**.

Peer Editor: _____ Date: _____

Author: _____ Work Title: _____

	Yes	No	Comment
1. Is there evidence of **prewriting** (brainstorming, planning)?			
2. Are the **title** main words **capitalized**?			
3. Does the **title fit** the work?			
4. Are **paragraphs used** to organize information?			
5. Is the **introduction** effective?			
6. Is the **main idea** clear, with a **sense of purpose**?			
7. Is information placed in **logical order**?			
8. Is there enough **supporting evidence**?			
9. Does the writer stay **on topic**?			
10. Is the writing **interesting**?			
11. Is the **word choice** appropriate?			
12. Does each **sentence begin** with **capital letter**?			
13. Does each **sentence end** with proper **punctuation**?			
14. Is each **sentence a complete thought**?			
15. Are there any **spelling errors** (**underline please**)?			
16. Are there other words that should be **capitalized**?			
17. Are **plurals** and **possessives** correct?			
18. Are **quotation marks** used correctly?			
19. Is the **conclusion** effective and relevant?			
20. Is **written text** well **organized** on paper?			
Other Comments			

PEER EDITING FORM

Ask a **classmate** to read through what you have written, check off the box next to each question, and write a brief comment that will help improve your work. Underlining and changes are permitted if done in **pencil**.

Peer Editor: _____ Date: _____

Author: _____ Work Title: _____

	Yes	No	Comment
1. Is there evidence of **prewriting** (brainstorming, planning)?			
2. Are the **title** main words **capitalized**?			
3. Does the **title fit** the work?			
4. Are **paragraphs used** to organize information?			
5. Is the **introduction** effective?			
6. Is the **main idea** clear, with a **sense of purpose**?			
7. Is information placed in **logical order**?			
8. Is there enough **supporting evidence**?			
9. Does the writer stay **on topic**?			
10. Is the writing **interesting**?			
11. Is the **word choice** appropriate?			
12. Does each **sentence begin** with a **capital letter**?			
13. Does each **sentence end** with proper **punctuation**?			
14. Is each **sentence a complete thought**?			
15. Are there any **spelling errors** (**underline please**)?			
16. Are there other words that should be **capitalized**?			
17. Are **plurals** and **possessives** correct?			
18. Are **quotation marks** used correctly?			
19. Is the **conclusion** effective and relevant?			
20. Is **written text** well **organized** on paper?			
Other Comments			

Peer Editing Form

Ask a **classmate** to read through what you have written, check off the box next to each question, and write a brief comment that will help improve your work. Underlining and changes are permitted if done in **pencil**.

Peer Editor: _____ Date: _____

Author: _____ Work Title: _____

	Yes	No	Comment
1. Is there evidence of **prewriting** (brainstorming, planning)?			
2. Are the **title** main words **capitalized**?			
3. Does the **title fit** the work?			
4. Are **paragraphs used** to organize information?			
5. Is the **introduction** effective?			
6. Is the **main idea** clear, with a **sense of purpose**?			
7. Is information placed in **logical order**?			
8. Is there enough **supporting evidence**?			
9. Does the writer stay **on topic**?			
10. Is the writing **interesting**?			
11. Is the **word choice** appropriate?			
12. Does each **sentence begin** with a **capital letter**?			
13. Does each **sentence end** with proper **punctuation**?			
14. Is each **sentence a complete thought**?			
15. Are there any **spelling errors** (**underline please**)?			
16. Are there other words that should be **capitalized**?			
17. Are **plurals** and **possessives** correct?			
18. Are **quotation marks** used correctly?			
19. Is the **conclusion** effective and relevant?			
20. Is **written text** well **organized** on paper?			
Other Comments			

Copyright © 2001, 2003, 2009 by Stevan Krajnjan

The Teacher's Binder

PROOFREAD iT!

Ask a classmate to read through what you have written, check off the box next to each question, and write a brief comment that will help improve your work. Underlining and changes are permitted if done in pencil.

Author: _____ Work Title: _____

	Yes	No	Comment
1. Is there evidence of **prewriting** (brainstorming, planning)?			
2. Are the title main words **capitalized**?			
3. Does the title fit the work?			
4. Are **paragraphs used** to organize information?			
5. Is the **introduction** effective?			
6. Is the **main idea** clear, with a **sense of purpose**?			
7. Is information placed in **logical order**?			
8. Is there enough **supporting evidence**?			
9. Does the writer stay **on topic**?			
10. Is the writing **interesting**?			
11. Is the **word choice** appropriate?			
12. Does each **sentence begin** with a **capital letter**?			
13. Does each **sentence end** with proper **punctuation**?			
14. Is each **sentence** a **complete thought**?			
15. Are there any **spelling errors** (*underline please*)?			
16. Are there other words that should be **capitalized**?			
17. Are **plurals** and **possessives** correct?			
18. Are **quotation marks** used correctly?			
19. Is the **conclusion** effective and relevant?			
20. Is **written text** well **organized** on paper?			

Other Comments

Copyright © 2001, 2003, 2009 by Stevan Krajnjan

The Teacher's Binder

Project Self-Evaluation

Name: _____

Date: _____

Project: _____

Part of this project that **makes me feel very proud** is	
Did I work as best as I could on this project? Explain.	
This is what I could have done **to improve** the quality of my work.	
The **reasons** why I **liked / disliked** working on this project:	
Here are some **suggestions** on how this project could be **improved** and made **more interesting**.	
The mark that I would give myself out of **10** is ... _____ **10** Please explain the reason.	

Copyright © 2001. 2003. 2009 by Stevan Krajnjan

Tracking Sheet

ASSIGNMENT: _____

Student Name					
					✓

Copyright © 2001. 2003. 2009 by Stevan Krajnjan

The Teacher's Binder

Tracking Sheet

ASSIGNMENT: _____

Student Name				
				✓

Copyright © 2001, 2003, 2009 by Stevan Krajnjan

Tracking Sheet

Student Name							
							✓

Copyright © 2001, 2003, 2009 by Stevan Krajnjan

Date: _____

MATH COMPUTATION TRACKING SHEET

Student Name	Place Value	SUBTRACTION −	ADDITION +	MULTIPLICATION ×	DIVISION ÷	FRACTIONS /

Copyright © 2001, 2003, 2009 by Stevan Krajnjan

Class Birthdays

Name	Date of Birth	Name	Date of Birth

Copyright © 2001, 2003, 2009 by Stevan Krajnjan

The Teacher's Binder

Leaving the Room?

Please sign out **in full**, and write **neatly**.

Date	Student Name	Time Out	Time In

Copyright © 2001, 2003, 2009 by Stevan Krajnjan

LEAVING THE ROOM ?

Date	Student Name	TIME OUT	Reason for Leaving	TIME IN

Copyright © 2001, 2003, 2009 by Stevan Krajnjan

The Teacher's Binder

Thank You!

To: _____

_____

_____

_____

Teacher: _____

Date: _____

THANK YOU!

To: _____

_____

_____

_____

Teacher: _____

Date: _____

THANK YOU!

To: _____

_____

_____

_____

Teacher: _____

Date: _____

Copyright © 2001, 2003, 2009 by Stevan Krajnjan

THANK YOU!

To: _____
_____
_____
_____

Teacher: _____
Date: _____

Thank You!

To: _____
_____
_____
_____

Teacher: _____
Date: _____

Thanks!

To: _____
_____
_____
_____

Teacher: _____
Date: _____

Copyright © 2001, 2003, 2009 by Stevan Krajnjan

NAME: _____

Subject	Work Missed	Completed (✓)

Copyright © 2001. 2003. 2009 by Stevan Krajnjan

WHILE YOU WERE AWAY...

You have **missed some school work** while you were away. To get caught up you need to do the following:

1. **Find out** what the class has done during your absence.
2. **Record** the work that needs to be completed on this sheet.
3. **Do** all assigned work as soon as possible.

Name: _____

Subject	Work Missed	Completed? (✓)
1.		◯
2.		◯
3.		◯
4.		◯
5.		◯

Copyright © 2001, 2003, 2009 by Stevan Krajnjan

 **Book**

Sign-Out Sheet

Sign your name below if you are **borrowing** a book from our class.

NAME	BOOK TITLE	Date Borrowed	Date Returned

Copyright © 2001. 2003. 2009 by Stevan Krajnjan

Materials

SIGN-OUT SHEET

NAME	What Was Borrowed	Date Borrowed	Date Returned

Copyright © 2001, 2003, 2009 by Stevan Krajnjan

The Teacher's Binder

Date: _____

Student Name: _____

Time of Incident: _____

Describe in detail **what happened and why,** in your opinion, it happened.

_____

_____

_____

_____

_____

_____

_____

_____

Did anyone else **see** what happened? _____

Was anyone **hurt**? _____

What **strategies** could have been used in order to **avoid** this incident?

Staff Comment: _____

_____

_____

_____

Staff **Signature:** _____

Parent Comment: _____

_____

_____

_____

Parent **Signature:** _____

Copyright © 2001, 2003, 2009 by Stevan Krajnjan

Date: _____

Student Name: _____

Time of Incident: _____

Describe in detail **what happened** and **why**, in your opinion, it happened.

_____

_____

_____

_____

_____

_____

_____

_____

_____

_____

_____

_____

Did anyone else **see** what happened? _____

Was anyone **hurt**? _____

What **strategies** could have been used in order to **avoid** this incident?

_____

_____

_____

_____

STAFF Notes: _____

_____

_____

_____

_____

_____

Copyright © 2001, 2003, 2009 by Stevan Krajnjan

The Teacher's Binder

Classroom Incident Report

_____ has been instructed to leave the classroom and go to the school office for:

✓   ✓

- repeated **failure to comply** ____
- speaking **disrespectfully** ____
- **refusing to** do class **work** ____
- use of **profanity** ____
- being continually **off-task** ____
- **disruptive** behavior ____
- **harassing** classmates ____
- **destroying** school/student property ____
- coming to class **unprepared** ____

- **arguing** with the teacher, talking back ____
- **leaving** the **classroom** without permission ____
- **refusing to leave** the classroom ____
- possession of a **weapon** ____
- wearing **inappropriate clothing** ____
- **wearing** clothing **inappropriately** ____
- physical **aggression**, **fighting** ____
- **endangering** the **safety** of others ____
- use of **threats** ____

Other : _____

Three warnings were given ____   The student cooperated and left immediately ____
The student did not cooperate and refused to leave _____

Teacher: _____ Date: _____ Time: _____ Period: _____

✂ – ✂

Classroom Incident Report

A quick NOTE

_____ has been instructed to leave the classroom and go to the school office for:

✓   ✓

- repeated **failure to comply** ____
- speaking **disrespectfully** ____
- **refusing to** do class **work** ____
- use of **profanity** ____
- being continually **off-task** ____
- **disruptive** behavior ____
- **harassing** classmates ____
- **destroying** school/student property ____
- coming to class **unprepared** ____

- **arguing** with the teacher, talking back ____
- **leaving** the **classroom** without permission ____
- **refusing to leave** the classroom ____
- possession of a **weapon** ____
- wearing **inappropriate clothing** ____
- **wearing** clothing **inappropriately** ____
- physical **aggression**, **fighting** ____
- **endangering** the **safety** of others ____
- use of **threats** ____

Other : _____

Three warnings were given ____   The student cooperated and left immediately ____
The student did not cooperate and refused to leave _____

Teacher: _____ Date: _____ Time: _____ Period: _____

Copyright © 2001, 2003, 2009 by Stevan Krajnjan

Office Referral Form

_____ has been **instructed to leave the classroom** and go to the school office.

Teacher: _____ Homeroom _____ Time Sent: _____ Time Arrived: _____

REASONS FOR REFERRAL:

- repeated failure to comply ____
- speaking disrespectfully ____
- refusing to do class work ____
- use of profanity ____
- being continually off-task ____
- disruptive behavior ____
- harassing classmates ____
- destroying school/student property ____
- coming to class unprepared ____

- arguing with the teacher, talking back ____
- leaving the classroom without permission ____
- refusing to leave the classroom ____
- possession of a weapon ____
- wearing inappropriate clothing ____
- wearing clothing inappropriately ____
- physical aggression, fighting ____
- endangering the safety of others ____
- use of threats ____

Other: _____

Comment: _____

_____

_____

STRATEGIES TRIED:

- Warnings ____
- Time-outs ____
- Change seating location ____
- Conference in the hall ____

- Positive reinforcement ____
- Privileges removed ____
- Parent interview ____
- Program modifications ____

Other: _____

CONCLUSION:

_____

_____

_____

_____

Copyright © 2001. 2003. 2009 by Stevan Krajnjan

Classroom Detention Form

You have received a classroom **detention** today. To help reflect on the incidents, and to have a record of it, you are asked to **fill out** this form.

Name: _____ Date: _____ Time of incident: _____

Which **classroom/school RULE** did you choose NOT to follow?

_____

_____

DESCRIBE in detail what happened.

_____

_____

_____

_____

_____

_____

_____

Tell **WHY** you did this.

_____

_____

_____

What could you have done **differently**?

_____

_____

_____

Teacher Comment:

_____

_____

Student Signature: _____ Teacher Signature: _____

Parent Signature: _____

Copyright © 2001, 2003, 2009 by Stevan Krajnjan

LIBRARY PASS

Library Pass

Class: _____

Student(s): _____

_____

Assignment: _____

_____ Sign: _____

Return to classroom at: _____

Left the library at: _____

Library Pass

Class: _____

Student(s): _____

_____

Assignment: _____

_____ Sign: _____

Return to classroom at: _____

Left the library at: _____

Library Pass

Class: _____

Student(s): _____

_____

Assignment: _____

_____ Sign: _____

Return to classroom at: _____

Left the library at: _____

Library Pass

Class: _____

Student(s): _____

_____

Assignment: _____

_____ Sign: _____

Return to classroom at: _____

Left the library at: _____

Library Pass

Class: _____

Student(s): _____

_____

Assignment: _____

_____ Sign: _____

Return to classroom at: _____

Left the library at: _____

Library Pass

Class: _____

Student(s): _____

_____

Assignment: _____

_____ Sign: _____

Return to classroom at: _____

Left the library at: _____

Copyright © 2001, 2003, 2009 by Stevan Krajnjan

Library Pass

LIBRARY PASS

Class: _____

Student(s): _____

_____

Assignment: _____

_____ Sign: _____

Return to classroom at: _____

Left the library at: _____

LIBRARY PASS

Class: _____

Student(s): _____

_____

Assignment: _____

_____ Sign: _____

Return to classroom at: _____

Left the library at: _____

LIBRARY PASS

Class: _____

Student(s): _____

_____

Assignment: _____

_____ Sign: _____

Return to classroom at: _____

Left the library at: _____

LIBRARY PASS

Class: _____

Student(s): _____

_____

Assignment: _____

_____ Sign: _____

Return to classroom at: _____

Left the library at: _____

LIBRARY PASS

Class: _____

Student(s): _____

_____

Assignment: _____

_____ Sign: _____

Return to classroom at: _____

Left the library at: _____

LIBRARY PASS

Class: _____

Student(s): _____

_____

Assignment: _____

_____ Sign: _____

Return to classroom at: _____

Left the library at: _____

Copyright © 2001. 2003. 2009 by Stevan Krajnjan

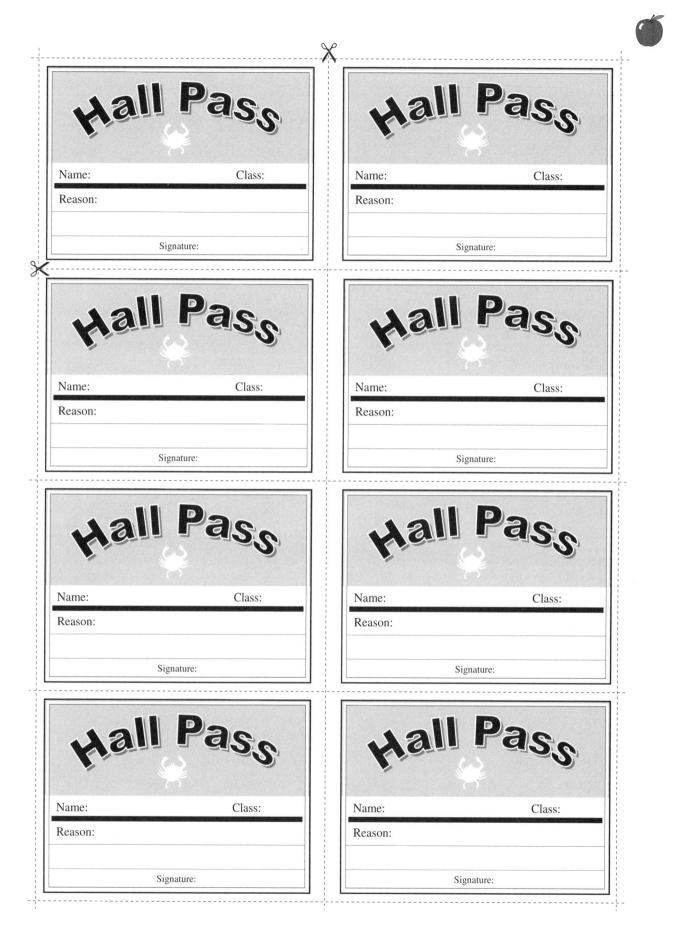

Hall Pass

Name: _____ Class: _____
Reason: _____
_____
Signature: _____

Hall Pass

Name: _____ Class: _____
Reason: _____
_____
Signature: _____

Hall Pass

Name: _____ Class: _____
Reason: _____
_____
Signature: _____

Hall Pass

Name: _____ Class: _____
Reason: _____
_____
Signature: _____

Hall Pass

Name: _____ Class: _____
Reason: _____
_____
Signature: _____

Hall Pass

Name: _____ Class: _____
Reason: _____
_____
Signature: _____

Hall Pass

Name: _____ Class: _____
Reason: _____
_____
Signature: _____

Hall Pass

Name: _____ Class: _____
Reason: _____
_____
Signature: _____

Copyright © 2001. 2003. 2009 by Stevan Krajnjan

The Teacher's Binder

Copyright © 2001. 2003. 2009 by Stevan Krajnjan

Hall Pass

HALL PASS

Name: _____ Class: _____

Teacher: _____

Time Out: _____ Time In: _____

Hall Pass

HALL PASS

Name: _____ Class: _____

Teacher: _____

Time Out: _____ Time In: _____

Hall Pass

HALL PASS

Name: _____ Class: _____

Teacher: _____

Time Out: _____ Time In: _____

Hall Pass

HALL PASS

Name: _____ Class: _____

Teacher: _____

Time Out: _____ Time In: _____

Hall Pass

HALL PASS

Name: _____ Class: _____

Teacher: _____

Time Out: _____ Time In: _____

Hall Pass

HALL PASS

Name: _____ Class: _____

Teacher: _____

Time Out: _____ Time In: _____

Hall Pass

HALL PASS

Name: _____ Class: _____

Teacher: _____

Time Out: _____ Time In: _____

Hall Pass

HALL PASS

Name: _____ Class: _____

Teacher: _____

Time Out: _____ Time In: _____

COMPUTER PASS

Name: _____ Class: _____

Is permitted to use the computer this period.

Signed: _____

COMPUTER PASS

Name: _____ Class: _____

Is permitted to use the computer this period.

Signed: _____

COMPUTER PASS

Name: _____ Class: _____

Is permitted to use the computer this period.

Signed: _____

COMPUTER PASS

Name: _____ Class: _____

Is permitted to use the computer this period.

Signed: _____

COMPUTER PASS

Name: _____ Class: _____

Is permitted to use the computer this period.

Signed: _____

COMPUTER PASS

Name: _____ Class: _____

Is permitted to use the computer this period.

Signed: _____

COMPUTER PASS

Name: _____ Class: _____

Is permitted to use the computer this period.

Signed: _____

COMPUTER PASS

Name: _____ Class: _____

Is permitted to use the computer this period.

Signed: _____

Copyright © 2001, 2003, 2009 by Stevan Krajnjan

The Teacher's Binder

The holder of this pass is entitled to **one period** of uninterrupted use of classroom **computer**.

Signed: _____

Copyright © 2001, 2003, 2009 by Stevan Krajnjan

Washroom Pass

WASHROOM PASS

Permission is granted to:

Name: _____ Class: _____

Signed: _____

Washroom Pass

WASHROOM PASS

Permission is granted to:

Name: _____ Class: _____

Signed: _____

Washroom Pass

WASHROOM PASS

Permission is granted to:

Name: _____ Class: _____

Signed: _____

Washroom Pass

WASHROOM PASS

Permission is granted to:

Name: _____ Class: _____

Signed: _____

Washroom Pass

WASHROOM PASS

Permission is granted to:

Name: _____ Class: _____

Signed: _____

Washroom Pass

WASHROOM PASS

Permission is granted to:

Name: _____ Class: _____

Signed: _____

Washroom Pass

WASHROOM PASS

Permission is granted to:

Name: _____ Class: _____

Signed: _____

Washroom Pass

WASHROOM PASS

Permission is granted to:

Name: _____ Class: _____

Signed: _____

Copyright © 2001, 2003, 2009 by Stevan Krajnjan

Bathroom Pass

BATHROOM PASS

Permission is granted to:

Name: _____ **Class:** _____
Signed: _____

Bathroom Pass

BATHROOM PASS

Permission is granted to:

Name: _____ **Class:** _____
Signed: _____

Bathroom Pass

BATHROOM PASS

Permission is granted to:

Name: _____ **Class:** _____
Signed: _____

Bathroom Pass

BATHROOM PASS

Permission is granted to:

Name: _____ **Class:** _____
Signed: _____

Bathroom Pass

BATHROOM PASS

Permission is granted to:

Name: _____ **Class:** _____
Signed: _____

Bathroom Pass

BATHROOM PASS

Permission is granted to:

Name: _____ **Class:** _____
Signed: _____

Bathroom Pass

BATHROOM PASS

Permission is granted to:

Name: _____ **Class:** _____
Signed: _____

Bathroom Pass

BATHROOM PASS

Permission is granted to:

Name: _____ **Class:** _____
Signed: _____

Copyright © 2001, 2003, 2009 by Stevan Krajnjan

Office Pass

OFFICE PASS

OFFICE PASS

Class: _____

Student Name: _____

_____

Reason: _____

_____ Sign: _____

Left the office at: _____

Returned to classroom at: _____

OFFICE PASS

Class: _____

Student Name: _____

_____

Reason: _____

_____ Sign: _____

Left the office at: _____

Returned to classroom at: _____

OFFICE PASS

Class: _____

Student Name: _____

_____

Reason: _____

_____ Sign: _____

Left the office at: _____

Returned to classroom at: _____

OFFICE PASS

Class: _____

Student Name: _____

_____

Reason: _____

_____ Sign: _____

Left the office at: _____

Returned to classroom at: _____

OFFICE PASS

Class: _____

Student Name: _____

_____

Reason: _____

_____ Sign: _____

Left the office at: _____

Returned to classroom at: _____

OFFICE PASS

Class: _____

Student Name: _____

_____

Reason: _____

_____ Sign: _____

Left the office at: _____

Returned to classroom at: _____

Copyright © 2001, 2003, 2009 by Stevan Krajnjan

Game Pass

Game Pass

This pass entitles _____ to a game session of _____ **minutes** in length.

Activity:_____

    Date Used: _____

Game Pass

This pass entitles _____ to a game session of _____ **minutes** in length.

Activity:_____

    Date Used: _____

Game Pass

This pass entitles _____ to a game session of _____ **minutes** in length.

Activity:_____

    Date Used: _____

Game Pass

This pass entitles _____ to a game session of _____ **minutes** in length.

Activity:_____

    Date Used: _____

Game Pass

This pass entitles _____ to a game session of _____ **minutes** in length.

Activity:_____

    Date Used: _____

Game Pass

This pass entitles _____ to a game session of _____ **minutes** in length.

Activity:_____

    Date Used: _____

Copyright © 2001, 2003, 2009 by Stevan Krajnjan

Free Time Pass

FREE TIME PASS

FREE TIME FREE TIME FREE TIME

This pass entitles_____

to _____ minutes of **FREE TIME.**

Date used: _____

Teacher Signature: _____

FREE TIME PASS

FREE TIME FREE TIME FREE TIME

This pass entitles_____

to _____ minutes of **FREE TIME.**

Date used: _____

Teacher Signature: _____

FREE TIME PASS

FREE TIME FREE TIME FREE TIME

This pass entitles_____

to _____ minutes of **FREE TIME.**

Date used: _____

Teacher Signature: _____

FREE TIME PASS

FREE TIME FREE TIME FREE TIME

This pass entitles_____

to _____ minutes of **FREE TIME.**

Date used: _____

Teacher Signature: _____

FREE TIME PASS

FREE TIME FREE TIME FREE TIME

This pass entitles_____

to _____ minutes of **FREE TIME.**

Date used: _____

Teacher Signature: _____

FREE TIME PASS

FREE TIME FREE TIME FREE TIME

This pass entitles_____

to _____ minutes of **FREE TIME.**

Date used: _____

Teacher Signature: _____

Copyright © 2001. 2003. 2009 by Stevan Krajnjan

Special Job Pass

Special Job

SPECIAL JOB ... SPECIAL JOB ...

This pass entitles_____
to perform a **special job**: _____
Job **Date**: _____
Teacher **Signature**: _____

Special Job

SPECIAL JOB ... SPECIAL JOB ...

This pass entitles_____
to perform a **special job**: _____
Job **Date**: _____
Teacher **Signature**: _____

Special Job

SPECIAL JOB ... SPECIAL JOB ...

This pass entitles_____
to perform a **special job**: _____
Job **Date**: _____
Teacher **Signature**: _____

Special Job

SPECIAL JOB ... SPECIAL JOB ...

This pass entitles_____
to perform a **special job**: _____
Job **Date**: _____
Teacher **Signature**: _____

Special Job

SPECIAL JOB ... SPECIAL JOB ...

This pass entitles_____
to perform a **special job**: _____
Job **Date**: _____
Teacher **Signature**: _____

Special Job

SPECIAL JOB ... SPECIAL JOB ...

This pass entitles_____
to perform a **special job**: _____
Job **Date**: _____
Teacher **Signature**: _____

Copyright © 2001. 2003. 2009 by Stevan Krajnjan

No Homework Pass

NO HOMEWORK! PASS

NO HOMEWORK … NO HOMEWORK …

This pass entitles_____
to a **NIGHT WITH NO HOMEWORK.**

Date Used: _____

Teacher **Signature**: _____

NO HOMEWORK! PASS

NO HOMEWORK … NO HOMEWORK …

This pass entitles_____
to a **NIGHT WITH NO HOMEWORK.**

Date Used: _____

Teacher **Signature**: _____

NO HOMEWORK! PASS

NO HOMEWORK … NO HOMEWORK …

This pass entitles_____
to a **NIGHT WITH NO HOMEWORK.**

Date Used: _____

Teacher **Signature**: _____

NO HOMEWORK! PASS

NO HOMEWORK … NO HOMEWORK …

This pass entitles_____
to a **NIGHT WITH NO HOMEWORK.**

Date Used: _____

Teacher **Signature**: _____

NO HOMEWORK! PASS

NO HOMEWORK … NO HOMEWORK …

This pass entitles_____
to a **NIGHT WITH NO HOMEWORK.**

Date Used: _____

Teacher **Signature**: _____

NO HOMEWORK! PASS

NO HOMEWORK … NO HOMEWORK …

This pass entitles_____
to a **NIGHT WITH NO HOMEWORK.**

Date Used: _____

Teacher **Signature**: _____

Copyright © 2001. 2003. 2009 by Stevan Krajnjan

Copyright © 2001. 2003. 2009 by Stevan Krajnjan

Classroom Supplies List

ITEM NAME	Product Number	Number Required	Urgent?	Purchased?
1.				
2.				
3.				
4.				
5.				
6.				
7.				
8.				
9.				
10.				
11.				
12.				
13.				
14.				
15.				
16.				
17.				
18.				
19.				
20.				
21.				
22.				
23.				
24.				
25.				
26.				
27.				
28.				
29.				
30.				
31.				
32.				

Copyright © 2001, 2003, 2009 by Stevan Krajnjan

The Teacher's Binder

Classroom Supplies List

ITEM NAME				
1.				
2.				
3.				
4.				
5.				
6.				
7.				
8.				
9.				
10.				
11.				
12.				
13.				
14.				
15.				
16.				
17.				
18.				
19.				
20.				
21.				
22.				
23.				
24.				
25.				
26.				
27.				
28.				
29.				
30.				
31.				
32.				

Copyright © 2001. 2003. 2009 by Stevan Krajnjan

Teacher Purchased & Owned Supplies

ITEM NAME				
1.				
2.				
3.				
4.				
5.				
6.				
7.				
8.				
9.				
10.				
11.				
12.				
13.				
14.				
15.				
16.				
17.				
18.				
19.				
20.				
21.				
22.				
23.				
24.				
25.				
26.				
27.				
28.				
29.				
30.				
31.				
32.				

Copyright © 2001, 2003, 2009 by Stevan Krajnjan

CLASSROOM SUPPLIES - TO GET ✓

ITEM NAME	Number Required	Urgent?	Purchased?
1.			
2.			
3.			
4.			
5.			
6.			
7.			
8.			
9.			
10.			
11.			
12.			
13.			
14.			
15.			
16.			
17.			
18.			
19.			
20.			
21.			
22.			
23.			
24.			
25.			
26.			
27.			
28.			
29.			
30.			
31.			
32.			

Copyright © 2001, 2003, 2009 by Stevan Krajnjan

CLASSROOM CONSUMABLES ORDER FORM

Teacher: _____ Room: _____ **Supplier**: _____ Order Date: _____

ITEM DESCRIPTION	Item Number	Quantity	Unit Price	Total Price	Item Received?
1.					
2.					
3.					
4.					
5.					
6.					
7.					
8.					
9.					
10.					
11.					
12.					
13.					
14.					
15.					
16.					
17.					
18.					
19.					
20.					
21.					
22.					
23.					
24.					
25.					
26.					
27.					
28.					
29.					
30.					
			Subtotal:		
			Tax:		
			Final **TOTAL**:		

Copyright © 2001, 2003, 2009 by Stevan Krajnjan

The Teacher's Binder

Publisher Order Form

BILL TO:

Name: _____

Address: _____
_____

City/Town: _____

Province/State: _____

Country: _____ Zip/Postal Code: _____

Telephone Number: ( ) _____

Fax Number: ( ) _____

E-mail Address: _____

SHIP TO:

Name: _____

Address: _____
_____

City/Town: _____

Province/State: _____

Country: _____ Zip/Postal Code: _____

Telephone Number: ( ) _____

Fax Number: ( ) _____

E-mail Address: _____

❑ Yes, place me on your catalog list.

PUBLISHER: _____ Telephone: _____

Address: _____ Fax: _____

Copyright © 2001, 2003, 2009 by Stevan Krajnjan

Product Number	Product Name	Quantity	Unit Price	Total

METHOD OF PAYMENT

❑ Bill Purchase Order # _____

❑ Check/Cheque (*enclosed*)

CREDIT CARD Information

❑ Personal Card ❑ Corporate Card ❑ MasterCard ❑ Visa

❑ American Express ❑ Discover

Credit Card Number: _____

Expiration Date _____

Subtotal	
Shipping & Handling	
TOTAL	
Sales Tax	
GRAND TOTAL	

❑ Additional page attached for more products

Purchase Order Form

BILL TO:

Name: _____

Address: _____

_____

City/Town: _____

Province/State: _____

Country: _____ Zip/Postal Code: _____

Telephone Number: ( ) _____

Fax Number: ( ) _____

E-mail Address: _____

SHIP TO:

Name: _____

Address: _____

_____

City/Town: _____

Province/State: _____

Country: _____ Zip/Postal Code: _____

Telephone Number: ( ) _____

Fax Number: ( ) _____

E-mail Address: _____

❏ Yes, place me on your catalog list.

PURCHASING FROM: _____ Telephone: _____

Address: _____ Fax: _____

Product Number	Product Name	Quantity	Unit Price	Total

METHOD OF PAYMENT

❏ Bill Purchase Order # _____

❏ Check/Cheque (*enclosed*)

CREDIT CARD Information

❏ Personal Card   ❏ Corporate Card   ❏ MasterCard   ❏ Visa

❏ American Express   ❏ Discover

Credit Card Number: _____

Expiration Date _____

Subtotal	
Shipping & Handling	
TOTAL	
Sales Tax	
GRAND TOTAL	

❏ Additional page attached for more products

Copyright © 2001, 2003, 2009 by Stevan Krajnjan

The Teacher's Binder

ONE DAY PROGRESS REPORT

Student's Name: _____

Teacher: _____ Class: _____

Date: _____

Period	Subject	Teacher Comment	Equipment in order? ✓ or ✗	Homework Assigned	Student Comment

Parent's Comment:

Signature: _____

Copyright © 2001, 2003, 2009 by Stevan Krajnjan

One Week Progress Report

Student's Name: _____ Class: _____

Teacher: _____

Week of: _____ to _____

Monday	Tuesday	Wednesday	Thursday	Friday

Parent's Comments	Parent's Comments	Parent's Comments	Parent's Comments	Parent's Comments
Signature:	Signature:	Signature:	Signature:	Signature:

Copyright © 2001. 2003. 2009 by Stevan Krajnjan

Copyright © 2001. 2003. 2009 by Stevan Krajnjan

One Week Progress Report

Student's Name: _____

Teacher: _____ Class: _____

Week of: _____ to _____

Monday	Tuesday	Wednesday	Thursday	Friday

Summary of progress:

Parent Comment:

Signature: _____ Date: _____

One Week Behavior

PROGRESS REPORT

Student's Name: _____

Teacher: _____ Class: _____

Week of _____ to _____

My **goals** for this week are:

1. _____

2. _____

3. _____

Place a ✓ in the appropriate box for each of the periods your goals have been **achieved.**

Student's Comments:

_____

_____

_____

_____

_____

_____

_____

_____

Period	1	2	3	4	5	6	7	8
Monday								
Tuesday								
Wednesday								
Thursday								
Friday								

Copyright © 2001, 2003, 2009 by Stevan Krajnjan

Student of the Week

_____ recognizes _____ Class: _____

For: _____

_____

Signed: _____ Dated: _____

✂ -

Student of the Week

_____ recognizes _____ Class: _____

For: _____

_____

Signed: _____ Dated: _____

Copyright © 2001, 2003, 2009 by Stevan Krajnjan

Certificate of Achievement

This certifies that

_____

has successfully

_____
_____
_____
_____

Signature

_____

Date

Copyright © 2001, 2003, 2009 by Stevan Krajnjan

Good Conduct Award

Awarded to:

Date

Teacher Signature

Copyright © 2001, 2003, 2009 by Stevan Krajnjan

Student of the Month

Presented to:

_____

Teacher Signature

_____

Date

Copyright © 2001. 2003. 2009 by Stevan Krajnjan

School Trip Notification

To parents/guardians of: _____

Event Description: _____

Where: _____

When: _____ Departure: _____ Return: _____

Method of Transportation: _____

The Purpose: *Students will . . .* _____

_____

_____

_____

Cost to Student: _____ Method of Payment: _____

Items Required: _____

Parent Volunteers Required: Yes ☐   Number: _____   No ☐

Other Information:

Supervising Staff: _____   _____   _____

Principal Signature: _____

✂ -

PLEASE RETURN THIS PORTION TO YOUR CHILD'S TEACHER BY _____

Trip: _____

I give ☐   **do not** give ☐ _____ permission to participate.

Yes, ☐ I would like to volunteer (*to be confirmed by teacher*).

Tel: _____   E-mail: _____   Cell: _____

_____
Parent/Guardian Signature

Copyright © 2001, 2003, 2009 by Stevan Krajnjan

School Trip Reflection

Draw and color **two** things that you remember from our recent class trip.

LOCATION: _____ Date: _____ Name: _____

WHAT DID YOU LEARN?

Copyright © 2001, 2003, 2009 by Stevan Krajnjan

Organize Ideas

Brainstorm, plan, and organize your main ideas <u>before</u> writing.

Name: _____

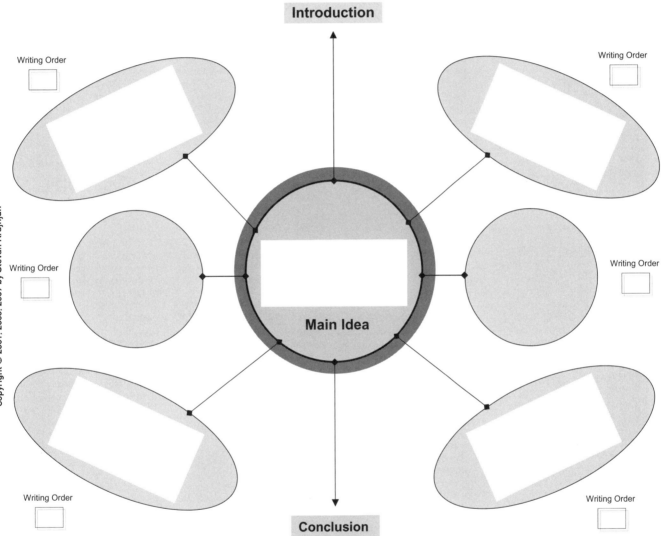

Introduction

Writing Order

Writing Order

Writing Order

Main Idea

Writing Order

Writing Order

Writing Order

Conclusion

Copyright © 2001, 2003, 2009 by Stevan Krajnjan

Brainstorm Ideas

Name: _____

Brainstorm and record **ALL** ideas as quickly as they come. Decide later whether they are useful or not.

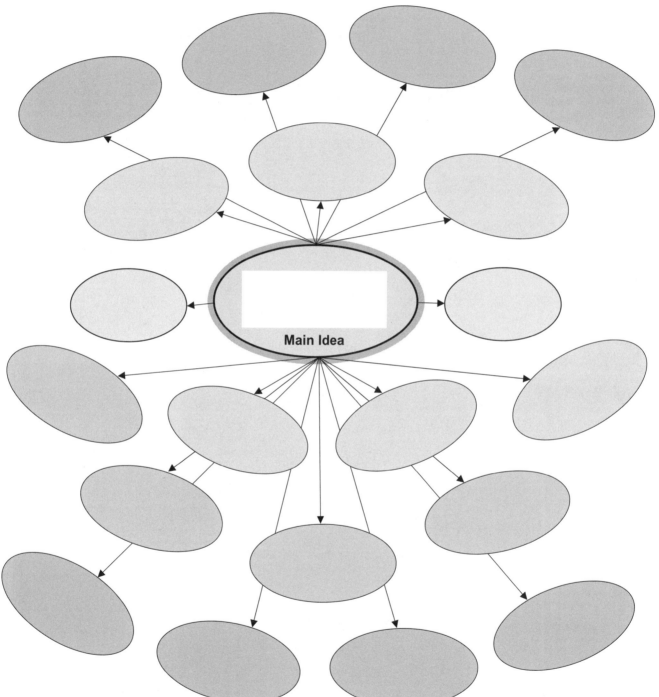

Main Idea

Copyright © 2001. 2003. 2009 by Stevan Krajnjan

The Teacher's Binder

Name: _____

Group the brainstormed ideas according to what they have in common.

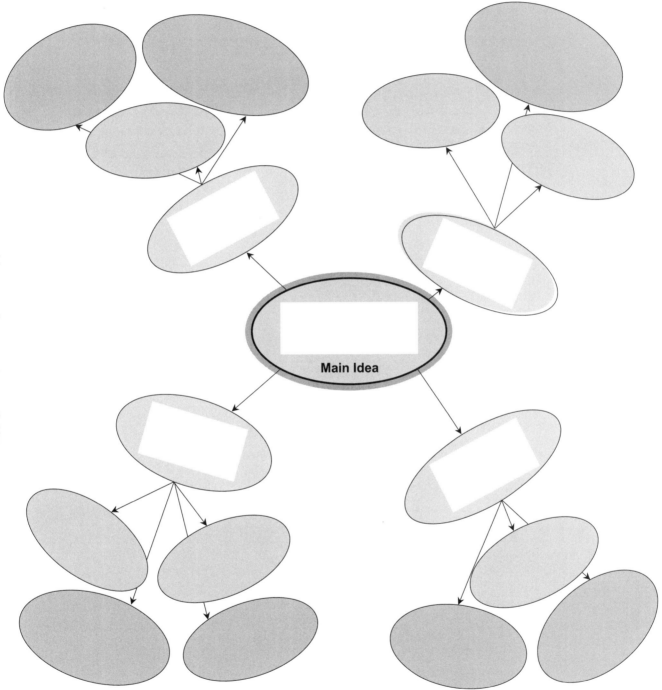

Main Idea

Copyright © 2001, 2003, 2009 by Stevan Krajnjan

Graphic Organizer

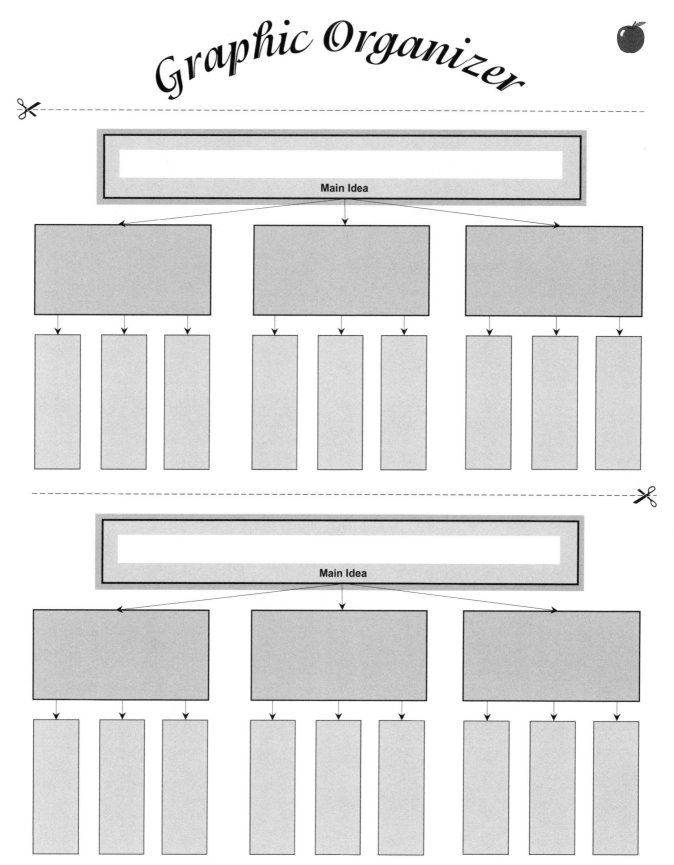

Main Idea

Main Idea

Copyright © 2001. 2003. 2009 by Stevan Krajnjan

Graphic Organizer

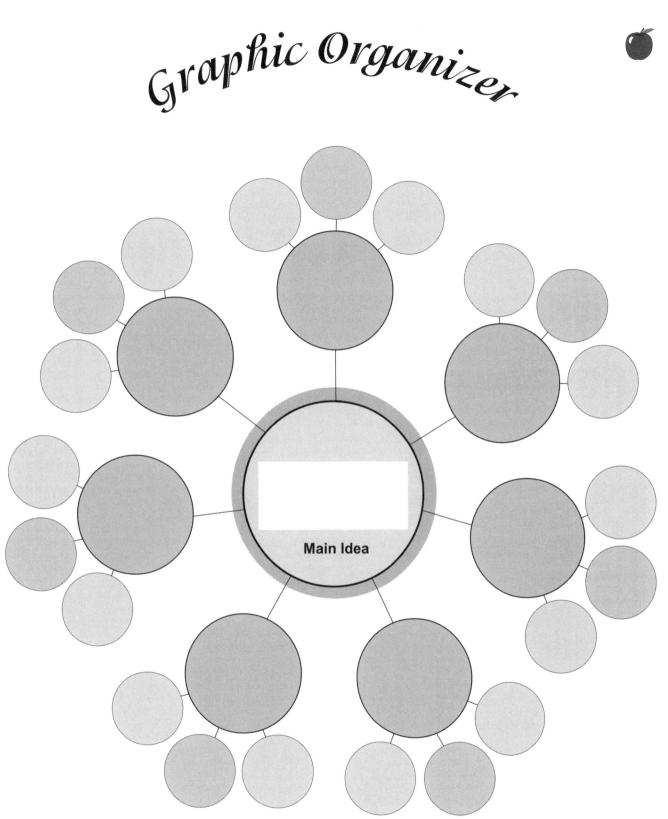

Main Idea

Copyright © 2001, 2003, 2009 by Stevan Krajnjan

Ideas in Sequence

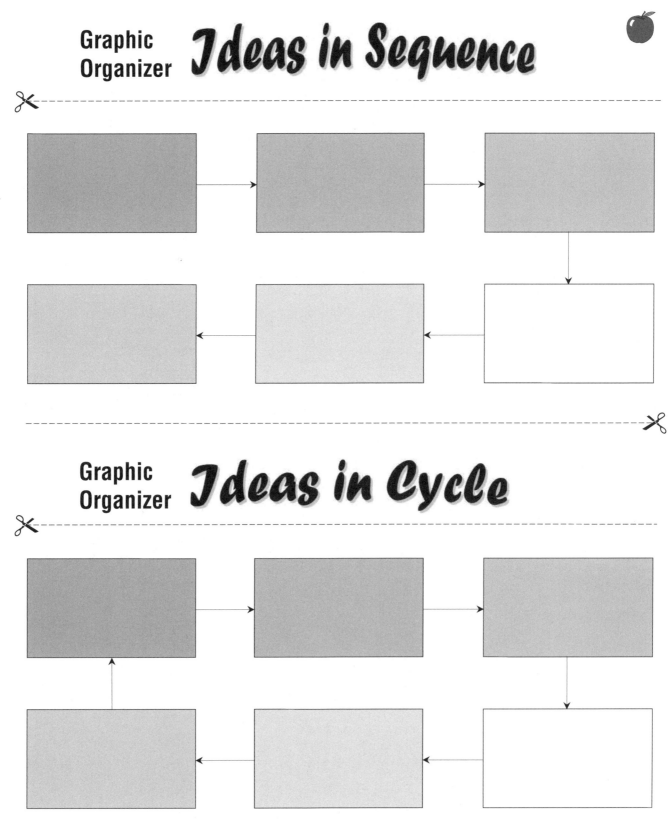

Ideas in Cycle

Copyright © 2001. 2003. 2009 by Stevan Krajnjan

The Teacher's Binder

Write a Simple Paragraph

Name: _____

Date: _____

TOPIC SENTENCE:

_____

Supporting Sentence **1**:

_____

Supporting Sentence **2**:

_____

Supporting Sentence **3**:

_____

Supporting Sentence **4**:

_____

Supporting Sentence **5**:

_____

CLOSING SENTENCE:

_____

WRITE THE PARAGRAPH

_____

_____

_____

_____

_____

_____

_____

_____

Copyright © 2001, 2003, 2009 by Stevan Krajnjan

Subject: _____

EVALUATION OF:

FINAL MARK =   =   % = [ ]

| Write a Paragraph | Name: _____ Parent Sig. _____ |

Achievement Level	R		1			2			3			4		
Letter Grade		R	$D\frac{1}{N}$	D	D+	$C\frac{1}{N}$	C	C+	$B\frac{1}{N}$	B	B+	$A\frac{1}{N}$	A	A+
Mark as (%)	Below 50%		50-52	53-56	57-59	60-62	63-66	67-69	70-72	73-76	77-79	80-84	85-89	90-100
Achievement Level	Remediation		Below			Low			Average			High		
Definition of Achievement Level	No evidence of expected knowledge and skill. Remediation is clearly needed.		Expected knowledge and skills have been demonstrated. In limited ways.			Some of the expected knowledge and skills have been demonstrated.			Most of the expected knowledge and skills have been demonstrated.			Expected knowledge and skills have been demonstrated clearly and effectively.		
Marks	0		1			2			3			4		
Performance	Very Limited		Limited			Inconsistent			Good			Excellent		

CRITERIA	Mark
Topic Sentence (*the beginning/introductory sentence*)	/
Additional Information (*details, inform about the topic*)	/
Summary (*the closing, concluding sentence*)	/
Conventions (*spelling, punctuation, grammar*)	/
TOTAL MARK:	

Comments:

Copyright © 2001. 2003. 2009 by Stevan Krajnjan

Subject: _____

EVALUATION OF:

FINAL MARK =   =   % = [   ]

Name: _____ Parent Sig. _____

Achievement Level	R		1			2			3			4		
Letter Grade	R		D⁻	D	D+	C⁻	C	C+	B⁻	B	B+	A⁻	A	A+
Mark as (%)	Below 50 %		50-52	53-56	57-59	60-62	63-66	67-69	70-72	73-76	77-79	80-84	85-89	90-100
Achievement Level	Remediation		Below			Low			Average			High		
Definition of Achievement Level	**No evidence** of expected knowledge and skill. **Remediation is** clearly needed.		Expected knowledge and skills have been demonstrated. **In limited ways**.			**Some** of the expected knowledge and skills have been demonstrated.			**Most** of the expected knowledge and skills have been demonstrated.			Expected knowledge and skills have been demonstrated clearly and effectively.		
Marks	0		1			2			3			4		
Performance	Very Limited		Limited			Inconsistent			Good			Excellent		

CRITERIA	Mark
TOTAL MARK:	

Comments:

Copyright © 2001. 2003. 2009 by Stevan Krajnjan

LINKING OR TRANSITION WORDS

Connect your ideas, phrases, and sentences, and make your writing flow by using **Linking** or **Transition** words.

To **INTRODUCE** a Paragraph
admittedly, assuredly, at this level, granted, generally speaking, in general, no doubt, nobody denies, obviously, to be sure, true, undoubtedly, unquestionably

To show **TIME or SEQUENCE**
after, afterward, as soon as, at, at first, at last, at once, at the same time, before, before long, during, eventually, finally, first, immediately, in the end, in the first place, in the meantime, last, later, meanwhile, next, now, presently, second, soon, then, third, today, tomorrow, until, while, when suddenly, yesterday

To show **ADDITION**
again, also, another, as well, at last, besides, finally, first, in addition, in conclusion, lastly, moreover, next, second

To show **CONTRAST**, Change in Reasoning
after all, although, but, even though, however, nevertheless, notwithstanding, on the contrary, otherwise, still, yet

To **COMPARE** Similar Ideas
also, and, in addition, in like manner, in the same way, likewise, moreover, on the other hand, similarly, while

To show **LOCATION**
above, across, adjacent to, against, among, around, at the same place, behind, below, beneath, beside, beyond, by, down, in back of, in front of, in the distance, inside, into, near, off, onto, on top of, opposite to, outside, over, straight ahead, throughout, to the right, under

To **CONCLUDE**
all in all, as a result, because, finally, hence, indeed, in brief, in final analysis, in final consideration, in the end, for this reason, to sum up, on the whole, in conclusion, lastly, on the whole, this, therefore, thus, so, to sum up

To show **EXAMPLE**
for example, for instance, in this manner, thus

To show **RESULT**
accordingly, consequently, hence, therefore, thereupon, thus, wherefore

To **RESTATE** a point
in other words, point in fact, specifically

To **CONTINUE** a Line of Reasoning
additionally, and, also, because, clearly, consequently, besides that, in addition, in the same way, in the light of . . . it is easy to see . . . it is obvious, following this further, furthermore, moreover, pursuing this further, then

To **EMPHASIZE** a point
again, especially, for this reason, in fact, to emphasize, to repeat, truly

Copyright © 2001, 2003, 2009 by Stevan Krajnjan

Copyright © 2001, 2003, 2009 by Stevan Krajnjan

Name: _____

Topic: _____

Word Search

1. _____
2. _____
3. _____
4. _____
5. _____
6. _____
7. _____
8. _____
9. _____
10. _____
11. _____
12. _____

13. _____
14. _____
15. _____
16. _____
17. _____
18. _____
19. _____
20. _____
21. _____
22. _____
23. _____
24. _____

Handwriting PAPER

Name: _____

Copyright © 2001, 2003, 2009 by Stevan Krajnjan

The Grid (5 cm)

Copyright © 2001, 2003, 2009 by Stevan Krajnjan

The Grid  (1 inch)

Copyright © 2001. 2003. 2009 by Stevan Krajnjan

The Teacher's Binder

 **The Grid** (2 cm)

Copyright © 2001, 2003, 2009 by Stevan Krajnjan

The Grid (1 cm)

Copyright © 2001. 2003. 2009 by Stevan Krajnjan

The Grid

(10 × 10 cm)

Copyright © 2001. 2003. 2009 by Stevan Krajnjan

10 BY 10 GRIDS

Copyright © 2001, 2003, 2009 by Stevan Krajnjan

The Teacher's Binder

The Grid (0.5 cm)

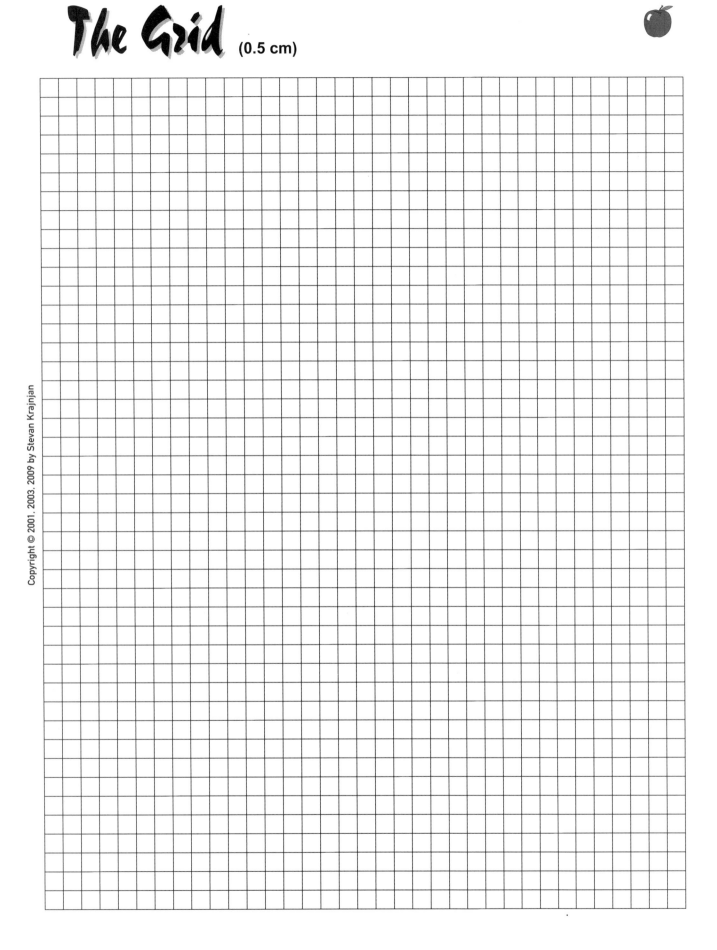

Copyright © 2001. 2003. 2009 by Stevan Krajnjan

The Grid  (0.5 cm - dotted)

Copyright © 2001, 2003, 2009 by Stevan Krajnjan

The Teacher's Binder

GRAPH PAPER

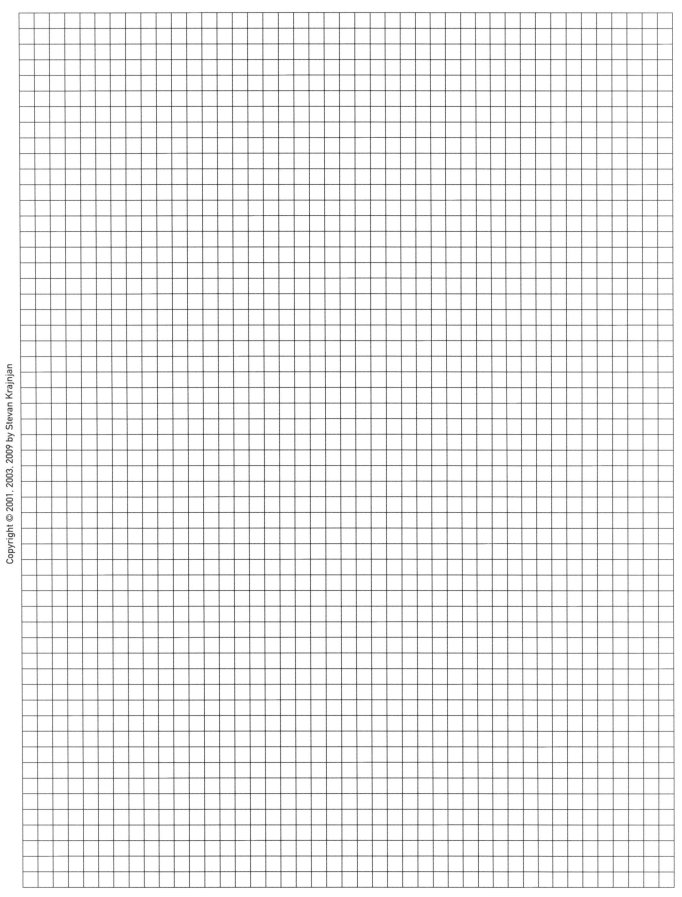

Copyright © 2001. 2003. 2009 by Stevan Krajnjan

GRAPH PAPER

Copyright © 2001, 2003, 2009 by Stevan Krajnjan

The Teacher's Binder

GRAPH PAPER

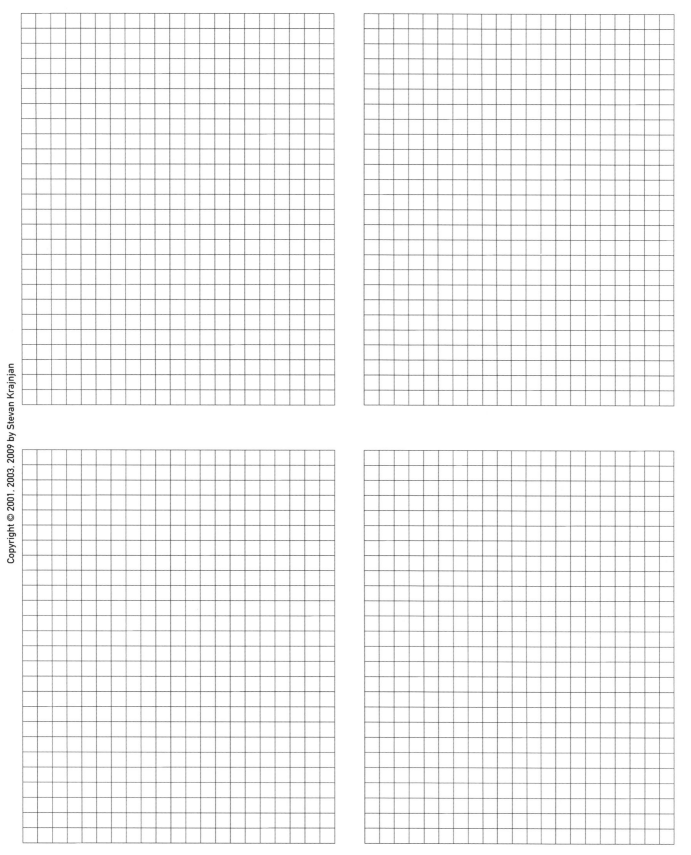

Copyright © 2001, 2003, 2009 by Stevan Krajnjan

GRAPH PAPER

Copyright © 2001. 2003. 2009 by Stevan Krajnjan

The Teacher's Binder

Square Dot Paper (1 cm)

Copyright © 2001, 2003, 2009 by Stevan Krajnjan

Square Dot Paper (0.5 cm)

Copyright © 2001, 2003, 2009 by Stevan Krajnjan

Positive Comment Strips

Use this activity to help build student self-esteem. Provide your students with one or more copies of this page and instruct them to write one **positive comment** about every person in the classroom on each of the outlined strips (*teacher included*). Emphasize that harmful comments are not appropriate and will be screened and discarded. When all comments are completed, they are to be cut into strips, handed in to you, inspected, collated, and stapled. Lastly, present your students with their own package of "feel good," positive comments and just watch the smiles!

Name	Comment:
Name	Comment:
Name	Comment:
Name	Comment:
Name	Comment:
Name	Comment:
Name	Comment:
Name	Comment:
Name	Comment:
Name	Comment:
Name	Comment:

> © 2009 | Copyright © 2001. 2003. 2009 by Stevan Krajnjan

DETENTION LOG

CLASSROOM

Teacher: _____   Room: _____

Date	Student Name	Offense	Parents/ Guardians Contacted?

Copyright © 2001, 2003, 2009 by Stevan Krajnjan

DETENTION LOG
STUDENT

Student: _____   Room: _____

Date	Offense	Parents Contacted?

Copyright © 2001, 2003, 2009 by Stevan Krajnjan

Notebook Expectations

- Write using a **blue pen.**
- **Underline titles** and dates using a pen and a ruler.
- **Capitalize** large words in all titles.
- **Write** on right hand side pages first.
- Do not **write/ draw/ scribble/ doodle** on any part of the cover.
- Keep your notebook **neat!.**

Notebook Expectations

- Write using a **blue pen.**
- **Underline titles** and dates using a pen and a ruler.
- **Capitalize** large words in **all titles.**
- **Write** on right hand side pages **first.**
- Do not **write/ draw/ scribble/ doodle** on any part of the cover.
- Keep your notebook **neat!.**

Notebook Expectations

- Write using a **blue pen.**
- **Underline titles** and dates using a pen and a ruler.
- **Capitalize** large words in all titles.
- **Write** on right hand side pages first.
- Do not **write/ draw/ scribble/ doodle** on any part of the cover.
- Keep your notebook **neat!.**

Notebook Expectations

- Write using a **blue pen.**
- **Underline titles** and dates using a pen and a ruler.
- **Capitalize** large words in all titles.
- **Write** on right hand side pages first.
- Do not **write/ draw/ scribble/ doodle** on any part of the cover.
- Keep your notebook **neat!.**

Notebook Expectations

- Write using a **blue pen.**
- **Underline titles** and dates using a pen and a ruler.
- **Capitalize** large words in all titles.
- **Write** on right hand side pages first.
- Do not **write/ draw/ scribble/ doodle** on any part of the cover.
- Keep your notebook **neat!.**

Notebook Expectations

- Write using a **blue pen.**
- **Underline titles** and dates using a pen and a ruler.
- **Capitalize** large words in all titles.
- **Write** on right hand side pages first.
- Do not **write/ draw/ scribble/ doodle** on any part of the cover.
- Keep your notebook **neat!.**

Copyright © 2001. 2003. 2009 by Stevan Krajnjan

The Teacher's Binder

Notebook Expectations

- ◆ _____
- ◆ _____
- ◆ _____
- ◆ _____
- ◆ _____
- ◆ _____

Notebook Expectations

- ◆ _____
- ◆ _____
- ◆ _____
- ◆ _____
- ◆ _____
- ◆ _____

Notebook Expectations

- ◆ _____
- ◆ _____
- ◆ _____
- ◆ _____
- ◆ _____
- ◆ _____

Notebook Expectations

- ◆ _____
- ◆ _____
- ◆ _____
- ◆ _____
- ◆ _____
- ◆ _____

Notebook Expectations

- ◆ _____
- ◆ _____
- ◆ _____
- ◆ _____
- ◆ _____
- ◆ _____

Notebook Expectations

- ◆ _____
- ◆ _____
- ◆ _____
- ◆ _____
- ◆ _____
- ◆ _____

Copyright © 2001. 2003. 2009 by Stevan Krajnjan

MATH NOTEBOOK EXPECTATIONS

1. Write in pencil, underline in ink.

2. Keep table of contents updated.

3. Date every new topic.

4. Underline using a ruler.

5. Number pages as you use them.

6. Draw/ scribble/ doodle only on the last few pages of the notebook.

7. Do calculations in the page margins.

8. Keep your notebook neat!.

MATH NOTEBOOK EXPECTATIONS

1. Write in pencil, underline in ink.

2. Keep table of contents updated.

3. Date every new topic.

4. Underline using a ruler.

5. Number pages as you use them.

6. Draw/ scribble/ doodle only on the last few pages of the notebook.

7. Do calculations in the page margins.

8. Keep your notebook neat!.

MATH NOTEBOOK EXPECTATIONS

1. Write in pencil, underline in ink.

2. Keep table of contents updated.

3. Date every new topic.

4. Underline using a ruler.

5. Number pages as you use them.

6. Draw/ scribble/ doodle only on the last few pages of the notebook.

7. Do calculations in the page margins.

8. Keep your notebook neat!.

MATH NOTEBOOK EXPECTATIONS

1. Write in pencil, underline in ink.

2. Keep table of contents updated.

3. Date every new topic.

4. Underline using a ruler.

5. Number pages as you use them.

6. Draw/ scribble/ doodle only on the last few pages of the notebook.

7. Do calculations in the page margins.

8. Keep your notebook neat!.

Copyright © 2001. 2003. 2009 by Stevan Krajnjan

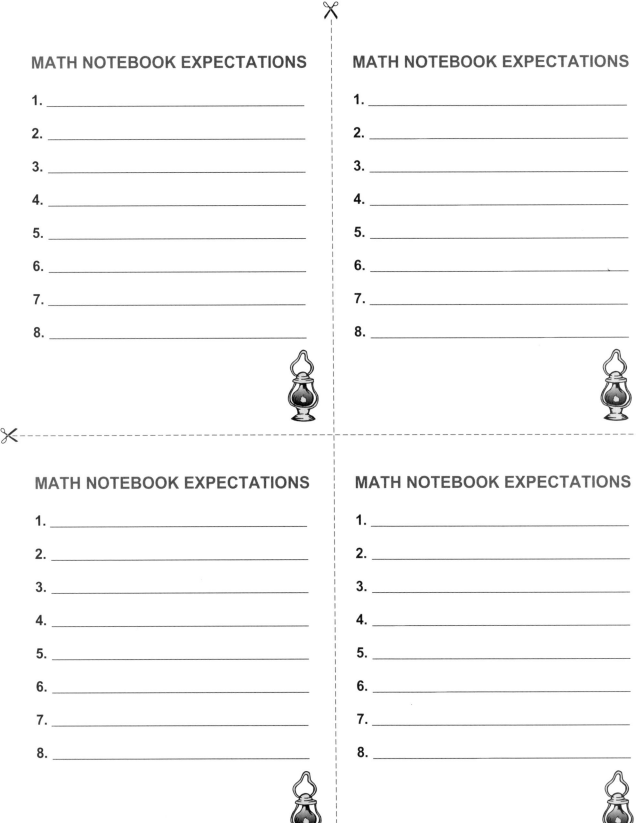

MATH NOTEBOOK EXPECTATIONS

1. _____
2. _____
3. _____
4. _____
5. _____
6. _____
7. _____
8. _____

MATH NOTEBOOK EXPECTATIONS

1. _____
2. _____
3. _____
4. _____
5. _____
6. _____
7. _____
8. _____

MATH NOTEBOOK EXPECTATIONS

1. _____
2. _____
3. _____
4. _____
5. _____
6. _____
7. _____
8. _____

MATH NOTEBOOK EXPECTATIONS

1. _____
2. _____
3. _____
4. _____
5. _____
6. _____
7. _____
8. _____

Copyright © 2001, 2003, 2009 by Stevan Krajnjan

Textbook Condition Form

Examine very carefully the textbook that was issued to you before you exit the classroom. Record in the table below any markings or defects that you see on the pages. **You will be held responsible for any defects not listed below**. The **replacement cost** for this textbook is: $_____.

Student: _____ Date of Issue: _____ Homeroom: _____

Title of Textbook: _____ Book Number: _____

Page	DESCRIPTION

Book condition **prior to issue**: New _____   Excellent _____   Good _____   Poor _____

Date of Return: _____   Condition **upon return**: Same: _____   Damaged _____   Lost Replacement Cost: $ ____

Copyright © 2001. 2003. 2009 by Stevan Krajnjan

Copyright © 2001, 2003, 2009 by Stevan Krajnjan

Copyright © 2001. 2003. 2009 by Stevan Krajnjan

The Teacher's Binder

Student Name:					

Copyright © 2001. 2003. 2009 by Stevan Krajnjan

Copyright © 2001, 2003, 2009 by Stevan Krajnjan

The Teacher's Binder

1.			
2.			
3.			
4.			
5.			
6.			
7.			
8.			
9.			
10.			
11.			
12.			
13.			
14.			
15.			
16.			
17.			
18.			
19.			
20.			
21.			
22.			
23.			
24.			
25.			
26.			
27.			
28.			
29.			
30.			
31.			
32.			

Copyright © 2001, 2003, 2009 by Stevan Krajnjan

Copyright © 2001. 2003. 2009 by Stevan Krajnjan

THINGS TO DO

✓

1.	
2.	
3.	
4.	
5.	
6.	
7.	
8.	
9.	
10.	
11.	
12.	
13.	
14.	
15.	
16.	
17.	
18.	
19.	
20.	

Copyright © 2001, 2003, 2009 by Stevan Krajnjan

THINGS TO DO

✓

1.	
2.	
3.	
4.	
5.	
6.	
7.	
8.	
9.	
10.	
11.	
12.	
13.	
14.	
15.	
16.	
17.	
18.	
19.	
20.	

Copyright © 2001, 2003, 2009 by Stevan Krajnjan

The Teacher's Binder

THINGS TO DO

1.
2.
3.
4.
5.
6.
7.
8.
9.
10.
11.
12.
13.
14.
15.
16.
17.
18.
19.
20.
21.
22.
23.
24.
25.
26.
27.
28.
29.
30.

Copyright © 2001, 2003, 2009 by Stevan Krajnjan

THINGS TO DO

THINGS TO DO

✓

	✓
1.	
2.	
3.	
4.	
5.	
6.	
7.	
8.	
9.	
10.	
11.	
12.	
13.	
14.	
15.	
16.	
17.	
18.	
19.	
20.	

	✓
1.	
2.	
3.	
4.	
5.	
6.	
7.	
8.	
9.	
10.	
11.	
12.	
13.	
14.	
15.	
16.	
17.	
18.	
19.	
20.	

Copyright © 2001. 2003. 2009 by Stevan Krajnjan

For additional and updated timesaving resource materials, please visit:
http://www.TimesaversForTeachers.com

The Teacher's Binder